An American Dream Comes True!
The World's Best BBQ Joint!

*Famous Dave's*

EAT ★ LAUGH ★ PARTY

*My whole purpose in life is to make you happy!*

*"My you always be surrounded by good friends and great barbeque!"*

*Famous Dave*

ISBN-13: 978-0-9892868-1-7

Digital edition published in 2013

eISBN: 978-0-9892868-0-0

Library of Congress Cataloging-in-Publication Data is available.

**Publisher:** Famous Dave Anderson

**Project Editor:** Claire Terrones

**Food Stylist:** Dave Anderson

**Food Stylist Assistants:** Kathy Anderson, Cathie Bowlby, Scott Barber, and Mark Lundeen

**Cover Design:** Dave Anderson, Lance Como, and Cory Johnson

**Book Design:** Dave Anderson and Cory Johnson

**Additional Design Consultation:** Doug Anderson and Deb Hatanpa

**Book Layout:** Dave Anderson, Lance Como and Cory Johnson

**Photography:** Mark Lundeen

**Photography Assistants:** Kathy Anderson, Cathie Bowlby, and Jacie Poitra

**Additional Photography:** Dave Anderson, Craig Bares, Gary Eckhart, Chuck Ryan, and Tim Steinberg

Printed in the United States

FAMOUS
DAVE
ANDERSON

www.BBQPartyCookbook.com

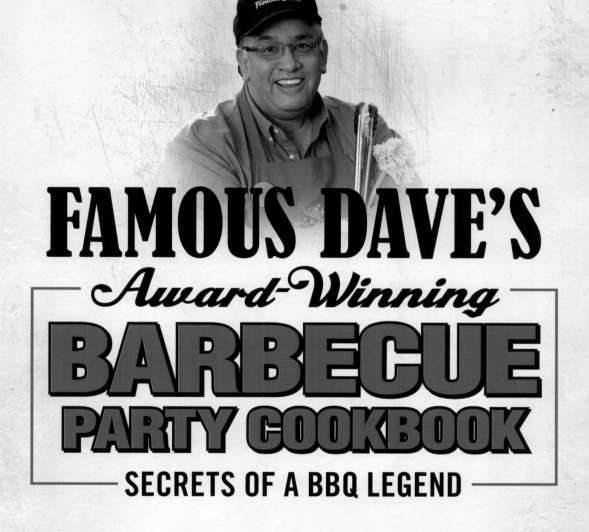

# FAMOUS DAVE'S
## *Award-Winning*
# BARBECUE
# PARTY COOKBOOK
### SECRETS OF A BBQ LEGEND

# EAT ★ LAUGH ★ PARTY

# EAT LAUGH PARTY!

### A Special Message From Famous Dave...

If you want everyone to leave your party, saying..."WOW what a fun party! We've never had so much fun and the food rocked the house!!! ...I am just dying to get my hands on a few of those recipes—they were so delish!" Then you're going to absolutely love my new BBQ Party Cookbook!

Most folks may be interested to know that my restaurants got their start from my rockin' & rollin' backyard BBQ parties. Before I ever opened up my first restaurant, I would invite my friends over for an old-fashioned backyard barbeque and would feed them new recipes that I was working on. I WOW'd them with my appetizers, my grilled and smoked meats, and fresh-from-the-oven desserts... and they would say, "Dave you just absolutely have to open up your own restaurant! Your cooking is amazing and the flavors are so robust... your restaurant is going to be a sure winner!"

Today, Famous Dave's is one of the fastest-growing barbeque restaurant companies in America, including winning over 700 Best of Class awards... more than any other restaurant in America, including the renowned restaurants in New York City or the famed celebrity chef restaurants in Las Vegas. You know what they say, "It ain't braggin' if it's the truth!" To say BBQ parties have made me who I am today, would be a huge understatement. In fact, I am proud to say, Nation's Restaurant News has declared Famous Dave's as one of "America's Hot Concepts!"

Throughout the years, many people have stopped me in my restaurant asking me for my barbecue secrets. So, by popular demand, I am sharing my best recipes that you can have fun serving to your family and friends at your next party, pignic, tailgate, or neighborhood shindig. Here's the most important thing about this cookbook...it is not just a book of recipes. Hopefully the process you go through to make these recipes will transform how you think about cooking in general. This cookbook is all about extracting the purest flavors out of each ingredient and then carefully "stacking flavors" to create the best tasting food possible. I know you're going to love my recipes, so... throw a party, have fun, and enjoy!

"May you always be surrounded by good friends and great barbeque!"

Rib-O-Liciously Yours,

*Famous Dave*

"Famous Dave" Anderson, Founder
Famous Dave's of America, Inc.
The World's Best BBQ Joint and America's Best Tasting Ribs!

# Welcome

# TO MY TABLE OF MOUTH-WATERING CONTENTS!

# The Importance of Brand-Name Ingredients

An important step to making a recipe taste great is understanding every ingredient that is used and how it enhances your recipe. Many cookbooks do not identify a brand name, which I think is unfortunate because a cook buying a brand name because of popularity or price… and not knowing the difference between quality and flavoring—does not understand how important ingredients are to a recipe.

Developing a taste library in your mouth and mind takes many years. In addition, I found there is no other way to fully remember the different seasonings as well as all the flavor nuances of different brand names, so it is important to take good notes. Selecting the right brand is as important as finding the right blend of spices. For instance there are two types of Worcestershire sauces that I keep in my pantry. Lea & Perrins is a very robust sauce that produces a "whole mouth" taste, and French's Worcestershire has a different flavor profile that I use in recipes where I need a flavor that subtly enhances my recipe.

## A

Accent®

Angostura® Bitters

## B

Ball® Fruit-Fresh® Produce Protector

Bob's Red Mill® Corn Meal

Bush's® Baked Beans

Bush's® Black Beans

Bush's® Great Northern Beans

B-V® Beef Broth and Sauce Concentrate

## C

Cabot Vermont® Extra Sharp Cheddar

Cabot Vermont® White Cheddar

Campbell's® Beef Consommé

Captain Morgan's® Spiced Rum

Carnation® Evaporated Milk

Chambord®

Coca-Cola®

Contadina® Tomato Paste

Country Time® Lemonade

Crisco®

Crystal Farms® Sharp Cheddar

## D

Dannon® Vanilla Yogurt

Dickenson® Black Raspberry Preserves

Dr. Pepper®

## F

Famous Dave's Devil Spit®

Famous Dave's Georgia Mustard Sauce®

Famous Dave's Rich & Sassy BBQ Sauce®

Famous Dave's Signature Spicy Pickles®

Famous Dave's Steak & Burger Seasoning®

Famous Dave's Sweet & Zesty BBQ Sauce®

Famous Dave's Texas Pit BBQ Sauce®

Fleischmann's® Pizza Crust Yeast

Frank's Red Hot® Sauce

French's® Yellow Mustard

## G

Girard's® Raspberry Dressing

Grand Marnier®

Grandma's Original Unsulphured Molasses®

Green Giant® White Shoepeg Corn

Green Giant® Sweet Corn Niblets

## H

Hellman's® Mayonnaise

Hillshire Farms® Smoked Sausage Ring

Hunt's® Crushed Tomatoes

Hunt's® Petite Diced Tomatoes

Hunt's® Tomato Paste

Hunt's® Tomato Puree

## I

Inglehoffer® Wasabi Horseradish

## J

Jack Daniel's Tennessee Whiskey®

Jiffy® Yellow Cake Mix

Jimmy Dean® Premium Pork Sausage

Johnsonville® Smoked Sausages

Johnsonville® Hot Italian Sausages

Johnsonville® Mild Italian Sausages

## K

Kahlua®
Kame® Hoisin Sauce
Karo® Corn Syrup
Kern's® Peach Nectar
Kikkoman® Soy Sauce
Knorr® Chicken Base
Knorr® Chicken Bouillon Cubes
Knorr® Dry Vegetable Soup Mix
Kraft® Creamy Poppy Seed Dressing

## L

Lea & Perrins New Thick Style Worcestershire Sauce®
Louisiana® Hot Sauce

## M

Maggi® Chicken Soup Base
Margaritaville® Margarita Mix
Mission® Tri-Color Tortilla Chips
Mitsukan® Seasoned Rice Vinegar
Mizkan Nakano® Original Seasoned Rice Vinegar
Morton's® Canning Salt
Mott's® Apple Juice

## N

Nestlé® Unsweetened Chocolate

## O

Open Pit® BBQ Sauce
Oreo® Cookies

## P

Pace® Medium Salsa
Pam® Non-Stick Cooking Spray
Pepperidge Farms Butter Chessman Cookies®
Philadelphia® Cream Cheese
Pickapeppa Sauce®
Pillsbury® Moist Supreme Cake Mix
Polaner® Apricot Preserves
Polaner® Blueberry Preserves
Progresso® Chicken Stock

## Q

Queso Fresco® Mexican Style Farmer's Cheese, Shredded

## R

Red Star® Platinum Baking Yeast
Ritz® Crackers

## S

Sam's Club® Chicken Base
Samuel Adams®
Slim Jim® Meat Sticks
Smart Balance® Rich Roast Creamy Peanut Butter
Smucker's® Apricot Preserves
Spice Islands® Old Hickory Smoked Salt
Spicy Hot V8® Juice
Sprite®
Superior Touch Better Than Bouillon Beef Base®

## T

Texas Pete's® Hot Sauce
Trader Joe's® Candied Walnuts

## V

V8® Juice

## W

Western® Dressing
White Lily® White Cornmeal
Wish Bone® Robusto Italian Dressing
Wright's® Liquid Smoke

7UP®

**FINDING THE RIGHT INGREDIENT:**
Any ingredient listed in this cookbook that is not found in your local grocery store can be ordered online. I know it's not always convenient, but please don't substitute ingredient brands unless you know the substitution is of the same quality and flavor. Enjoying a great tasting recipe is worth the extra effort of finding the right ingredient. All Famous Dave's BBQ sauces and seasonings can be ordered online at: www.famousbbq.com.

# FAMOUS DAVE'S
## *Creating a Famous*
# BBQ PARTY
### THE PASSION IS IN THE DETAILS

# EAT ★ LAUGH ★ PARTY

# EAT LAUGH PARTY!

## *Pignics • Barbeques • Street Dances*

All across America, families can't wait for any excuse to get together with family & friends because then it's time to roll out the grill and it's time to party! Summertime barbecues are an American tradition of good old fashioned fun with family and friends. Whether it's a village street dance, country jam fest, family reunion pignic, or neighborhood block party… we all like to enjoy butt-rockin' music, cold beer, and great-tasting barbeque to celebrate good times and good friends!

*"My whole purpose in life is just to make you happy!"*
~Famous Dave Anderson

11

# 15 Tips
## for Planning the Most Memorable Party Ever!!!

**1** Great parties don't just happen; they take extra work and need to be well planned and executed. Make sure you have enough time to get things done.

**2** Rehearse your party weeks in advance. Set up wherever you are going to be serving the food and brainstorm how you can create the most imaginative way to serve your food.

**3** Make sure your guests can find your party! Great directions take the stress away from your guests having to find your party while trying to arrive on time. Here's a great tip: include your GPS coordinates on the invitation!

**4** I learned from my successful restaurant experience… if you impress all 5 senses of your guests, you will have a very memorable party. You need to envision everything in your guests' perspective from the moment they arrive to the time they leave. Ask yourself: What will they see when they drive up? How are they greeted? What will they do when they walk in…stand? get a drink? sit down? What music will they hear? How will you get them to mingle? Will they smell a wonderful aroma when they walk in your front door? How will they sit at the table? What will they taste? What will they do after they eat? What will they see if they use your bathroom? How will you signal them it's time to leave?

**5** What your guests see and remember are called "Guest Touch Points." These are the "moments of truth" that create a good impression, no impression, or a bad impression. A good host spends weeks thinking about each guest touch point at their party. A great host creates strategies for making the best impressions possible and writes out a plan for each strategy. This is how you create raving loyal fans of your parties!

**6** They say the devil's in the details. I say God is in the details or in this case… the party gods! It's the details that turn a get-together into a party that everyone raves about all over town. Be a great note-taker and write down everything, no matter how small your idea or thought. Sometimes it's simple details like fresh flowers in the bathrooms that people remember.

**7** This goes without saying… total cleanliness is very important. Start cleaning weeks in advance; don't underestimate the power of clean!

**8** Outdoor parties require contingency plans in case of bad weather. Having a number of pop-up gazebos or large umbrellas outfitted with party lighting makes for a lot of fun whether it rains or not. An outdoor party must… the day before your party, spray the yard for bugs and mosquitoes. A bug-free party makes all the difference in the world. It goes without saying, use an earth-friendly bug spray or have your yard professionally done…it is worth the extra effort!

**9** Fun parties don't always need main entrees. A bunch of appetizers for guests to munch on is often all it takes to have a successful get-together!

**10** Music is very important! Don't just turn on a radio or put on a CD. With today's technology, I hand pick every song with a beat that makes my guests comfortable while at my party. Have your music start off somewhat slow in the beginning; as people get over their inhibitions and start moving around and mingling, the beats of your song list should pick up. Program your mp3 player with your best party songs. Have a song list ready; many times people ask me how I put together such a great list of their most favorite songs. Remember, great beats make great party vibes!

**11** Disposable paper plates and napkins are great, but don't be a scrooge and buy the cheapest white plates you can find. Online you can find the best decorative, fun-themed paper plates, and napkins that turn your food into fun festive morsels of deliciousness worthy of the party gods!

**12** The party planning item most often overlooked… wastebaskets big enough to handle the size of your party. Decorate these to fit the theme of your party and have enough of them in easily accessible, plain sight areas. I can't tell you how many empty soda cans, paper plates, etc.,… we find weeks later in the oddest places in our home or backyard. I have to wonder what these people were doing at my party, and what they were thinking when they disposed of their empty cans and soiled napkins in these odd places...

**13** Do something really memorable... set up a photo opportunity. Decorate a corner of the room in your party theme complete with props. Next, take digital pictures of guests at your photo booth using a camera set up on a tripod. Have your computer set up with a printer, so you can take fun pictures of you with your guests and print them immediately. Print two sets of a photo; paste one in a scrapbook and let your guests write comments under their picture for an amazing party keepsake! While your guests are writing in your album, place the second photo in a frame and send your guests home with a ready-to-display keepsake of your party. (You can purchase really inexpensive frames from a dollar store.) You won't believe how much fun this can add to your party!

**14** Make your next party over-the-top! There are so many party websites that can create unique decorations for your next party. For instance there is a website where you can submit a digital photo and they create a life-size cutout of the person you're celebrating. Another fun idea: custom-themed party banners.

**15** Have chilled water on hand in appropriate themed containers. I love to use decorative drink dispensers with plenty of ice available for guests. What makes this fun is spiking the water with fresh orange and lemon slices. This beats providing bottled water and the resulting landfill trash… after all it's important to be "earth friendly!"

# CREATIVE IDEAS TO GIVE YOUR PARTY A "WOW FACTOR"

## Personalized Invitations

Create your own fun and personalized party invitation! With today's amazing digital printing capabilities, you can create really fun invites without having to spend a small fortune. When your friends receive a hand-created invitation, it makes the invite more friendly and personable. Here I scanned an American Flag bandana for the background. Next, I created my invite information centerpiece which I printed on the flag-designed paper. Without much effort, and in no time at all… I have my own personalized party invite. You can also use a variety of printed papers or fabrics to scan backgrounds for different themed parties. It's a simple idea that's fun and affordable!

## Great Party Décor & Quick Service Ideas

Dress up your party table! Varying heights make a table more interesting. Here I used wooden soda pop cases and wrapped them in bandanas. Don't be afraid to use big fun props to create centers of attention… like the kid's antique car that I used as my cornbread holder. Colorful flower displays always add fun to any table.

Get a book on food garnishing. You can really jumpstart a platter with decorative garnishes made out of real food. Creating fun garnishes to dress up your party platters are the subtle "wow factors" that get people talking about your party.

## First Impressions Create The Party

Even if it's only a backyard party for your own family… never pass up an opportunity to dress up the table. Little things that mean something to you or your family work perfectly. Since this is a backyard BBQ party, I thought it was a good occasion to bring out my "Best BBQ Sauce In America" trophy!

Use a variety of different colored plates, bowls, boxes, and fabrics to create interest on your table. I like to place fresh ingredients on the table like onions, green peppers, strawberries, or whatever was used in creating the menu. Seeing fresh ingredients creates an unforgettable impression of made-from-scratch cooking and that you care about the food you cook. Please, Please, Please… don't just set bowls down on a table. A little color, height, and decoration will create a party spread no one will forget!

*Hors d'oeuvres are sometimes described as Mystery Meat and that will get on any host's "n'oeuvres!" Never wanting that to happen to me, I devoted my cooking passion to creating great-tasting grilled & barbecued party foods. I believe everyone should know exactly what goes into their mouths...that's when they started calling me "Famous."*

~Famous Dave Anderson

15

## Bandana-Wrapped Silverware

Wrap your silverware or plastic throwaways in colorful bandanas. It adds color to your party spread and is one of those touches your guests will remember.

## Sandwich Display Ideas!

It's easy to pile up sandwiches on a platter, but don't take the easy way out. Figure out fun ways to display your sandwiches and make your party the one everyone talks about all over town. Simple ideas like using mini-grills are a fun way to feature your BBQ sandwiches. Sometimes you need toothpicks to hold big sandwiches together... make sure you use creative fun picks that turn everyday sandwiches into feature attractions!

## Lemon Hand Cleaners

The only way to eat great barbecue is with your hands. Provide your guests with warm lemon fresh scented towels. Here I folded and rolled fun party cloth napkins. Next, I soaked them in warm water and topped them with fresh lemons. Your guests will appreciate a little touch of freshness!

## A Towering
## Barbecue Sauce Fountain

Back in Roman times, the orgies of gluttony really started when the wine began flowing out of their water fountains. Get your barbecue party started by throwing out the old fondue forks and turning your chocolate fountain into a love fountain for barbecue sauce. Your guests will go bonkers slathering their bones in this waterfall of barbecue sauce goodness!

## Famous Dave's
## Hot Tips!

Textured BBQ sauces will clog up the fountain. So to keep the love flowing, remember to use a smooth-texture barbecue sauce like Famous Dave's Rich and Sassy! Also from time to time, depending on how long the fountain runs during the party, the sauce will get thicker from water evaporating. You may have to add water to thin out the sauce.

17

# PARTY LIGHTING

## Creating a Magical Glow

Creating a magical glow at night can make your evening party unforgettable! Use hanging lights or candle lanterns to create a romantic magical flicker that only a real flame can provide.

## Theme Rope Lighting

Lighting can add a lot of fun and make your displays "sparkle!" Here I use "Piggy Lights" to wrap in and around my table display. These novelty lights come in a variety of fun themes like: palm trees and fish for beach-themed parties, cactus and sombreros for Mexican-themed parties, and footballs and soccer balls for sports-themed parties. Or get out your Christmas tree lights and wrap them around your displays for instant party sparkle!

## Lighting for the Whole Room

There are 5 types of party lighting used to decorate this party room.

1. Multi-colored icicle Christmas lights under the table skirting draw your guests into the table.

2. Lighted crystal garland beads wind their way around on top of the table.

3. Candle lanterns placed throughout the room create that special flickering effect.

4. Mini-white Christmas lights under the umbrella.

5. Big lighted multi-colored paper balls to decorate the perimeter of the room pulling everything together.

# PINEAPPLE: The Perfect Party Fruit

**Pineapples are probably the most versatile fruits for a party!** The fruit can be eaten, the shell used as a container, the juice used as a sweetener in drinks and sauces, and almost every part of the pineapple can be used as a garnish. I love fresh pineapple slices, grilled pineapple slices, or little wedges to spice up a party platter, but preparing the fresh pineapple can be a real chore by hand. A pineapple corer is an easy way to remove the skin and core... with a couple of quick twists you have beautiful, cored pineapple slices without all the hassle!

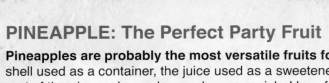

There is no comparison to the incredibly fresh taste of a real pineapple. Fresh pineapples are so readily available and easy to prepare... don't even think of buying pineapple in a can again! I believe canned pineapple ruins your recipe. Slice, dice, or chop your own fresh pineapples and your food will be incredibly better tasting!

## Pineapples as Carved Centerpieces

Pineapples have a natural spiral to their covering (the rind) and just removing the alternate spiral will create a striking garnish to any food presentation or party table.

## Grilled Pineapples

Pineapple can be grilled as a slab or sliced into wheels. Before grilling any pineapple, take a cloth dipped in vegetable oil and wipe the grill grates so the pineapple won't stick. This is important, as the sugars in the pineapple will caramelize and stick to the grill grates. Pineapple is a fruit that breaks apart easily,s so use a spatula when removing any pineapple from the grill.

## Pineapple Exotic Beverage Holders

Outside of empty coconut shells there isn't a more creative way to serve all sorts of crazy, fun beverages than in an empty pineapple! Collect all sorts of fun novelty items that can be used to garnish these exotic drinks. Some items you have to find in the kid's section of a variety store, like fun straws. Party picks and paper parasols are often found in the cocktail section of a liquor store. Here you can see I even used the pineapple leaves as a garnish.

## Pineapple as Food & Dip Containers

I like using the empty pineapple shell as a bowl with salsas, guacamoles, fruits, or crab salads. Brush the inside of the pineapple shell with a wash of Ball Fruit Fresh Protector to keep it from browning too rapidly.

# FAMOUS DAVE'S GRILLING GUIDE

"If there's *NO WOOD...* it ain't *NO GOOD!*"

# GRILLS & SMOKERS

## CHARCOAL GRILLS

I LOVE charcoal grills because they add real char and smoke flavors to your food, which is why you are grilling outdoors in the first place! Here's a tip… loosely wrap wet chunks of hickory or apple wood in aluminum foil and place it right on the hot briquettes or lump charcoal. Lump charcoal actually burns hotter than briquettes and is best for steaks. When using a charcoal grill DO NOT USE LIGHTER FLUID! Use a charcoal chimney as your starter. You can find charcoal chimneys wherever grills are sold. See *BBQ Party Tools* (pg. 29).

## TURNING YOUR CHARCOAL GRILL INTO A SMOKER

Turn your charcoal grill into a smoker by putting water-soaked wood chips in a metal tray or wrapping wet wood chips in aluminum foil. Loosely wrap wet wood chips of hickory or apple wood, in doubled-up aluminum foil and poke a few small holes in the foil. Place your smoker packets right on the hot briquettes or lump charcoal. Don't make the holes too big or your chips will catch fire. You don't want flames in your packet. You only want the wood to smolder; your most tasty flavors will come from the smoke.

## GAS GRILLS

Even though I prefer a live fire and smoke, gas grills are fine for searing steaks, hamburgers, and hot dogs. If you have a gas grill… I recommend getting a rotisserie. I especially love using a rotisserie for chickens, rib roasts, or large tenderloins.

**GAS GRILL HOT TIP:** Keep a spare propane tank handy, so you don't run out of gas while grilling. Better yet… if you use your gas grill all time, have the gas company hook it up to your home's natural gas line with a handy removable connecting jack. The gas valves on the grill will have to be changed, and the gas company can do this as well. You will love never running out of propane when you are cooking up a storm for your backyard party!

## FIRE PITS

I love a real fire of wood, usually oak or hickory, but any hard wood will work. Don't ever use pine, the smoke leaves an awful flavor. There's something about steaks, burgers, and sausages seared over a smoky live fire that makes them taste amazing. When the fat and juices drip down, the fire flares up and flame kiss the meat with incredible flavors.

## SMOKERS

Today, many small home smokers are available; these home smokers do a pretty good job of smoking your meats and fish. These home smokers are fairly inexpensive, and will give you many memorable meals.

## BIG GREEN EGG

I am often asked which is my favorite smoker, I guess at the top of the line… it has to be the large Big Green Egg. You just can't do any wrong with this smoker and I have gotten my best, most tender smoky meats out of the Big Green Egg. You have to dream about this one or have a very special Santa as it is no doubt an investment, but happy friends and family make this well worth the investment!

## MEADOW CREEK

I am also in love with my Meadow Creek Box Smoker. For me this is "old school" smoking where the live smoldering coals are directly under the meats. It's a bit more expensive, but perfect if you do a lot of backyard parties or tailgating! I have two grates for this smoker… one for regular smoking and the chicken grate. I especially love the chicken grate because it can be flipped over without having to move all the chicken pieces, which is perfect for doing large amounts of smoked chicken wings!

Meadow Creek Smoker with a chicken grate

24

# GETTING STARTED

You've got your grill and now you're ready to throw a Barbecue Party. The secret to a better barbecue begins with quality meat...

## GET TO KNOW YOUR LOCAL BUTCHER

If I am going to throw a fantastic backyard barbecue bash that's totally memorable, fun, with great tasting food... I am fanatical about starting out with the best cuts of meat that I can find. Your local butcher can get you the best cuts of freshly butchered meats that will WOW your party guests. I can't begin to tell you how many times my party guests have asked me where I get my meats... and I am happy to tell them about my local butchers at my favorite grocery store. I guarantee you these butchers know whenever I am in their grocery store!

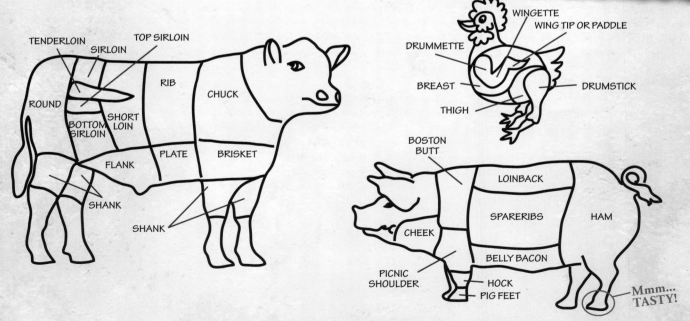

*"Growing up, we didn't have much, but for the longest time*
*I used to think that pig's feet was all the meat there was on a pig!"*
~Famous Dave

25

## PREPPING THE GRILL

After your clean grate has heated up, take a clean rag or folded-up paper towel and dip it into some cooking oil. Then, holding your paper towel with your tongs, wipe the grate with oil and immediately place your food on the grill. The greased grate helps prevent your food from sticking.

## CHARCOAL BRIQUETTES

A good rule when grilling (not smoking) is to plan for approximately 80 charcoal briquettes, which fills a large charcoal chimney. This covers 2/3 of the average-sized 22" grill.

## BRING MEATS TO ROOM TEMPERATURE

For the best results when grilling, bring your refrigerated meats to room temperature. This allows for a more even temperature throughout your meat. Larger or thicker cuts of meats will remain cooler in the center if the meat is still cold when placed on the grill. Marinate or season your meats while you are waiting for the meat to reach room temperature.

## DIRECT HEAT VS. INDIRECT HEAT

Direct heat is best for searing meats such as steaks, burgers, and hot dogs. Indirect heat is best for larger cuts of meat that you want to infuse with a smoky flavor. Indirect heat is created when you pile your charcoal to one side of the grill and place your meat on the opposite side of the heat. You can place an aluminum tray directly under your meat to catch any drippings. Depending on the cut of the meat you may want to put a liquid in the tray to provide moisture for leaner cuts of meat. Indirect cooking requires you to keep your grill cover on, and add more charcoal periodically. In the beginning, you are using about half as many briquettes since your objective is "low heat and slow cooking" versus a quick sear.

**DIRECT HEAT**

**INDIRECT HEAT**

26

## FLAMES, CHAR, and SMOKE

I believe man has a primal need to eat charred meat… there's something about chewing charred meat off a bone that brings out your inner caveman! There isn't anything better than meat that has been flame-kissed or slowly smoked over smoldering embers and coals. There's good barbecue wisdom in the old saying, "If there's no wood… it ain't no good!" There are many ways to add char or smoke flavor to a meat or veggie; everything from charcoal briquettes and lumps of charcoal to mesquite wood for steaks and hickory, apple or peach wood for pork and chicken.

My wood pile of hickory, maple, oak, and apple wood

You can buy wood chunks at most stores in the grilling section

## Soaking Large Chunks of Wood— Don't Bother!!! …It doesn't work.

This is a large six-inch chunk of hickory, which I soaked for 24 hours. As you can see, when I chopped the chunk in half, the water only penetrated about 1/8 inch into the wood. Large chunks of wood just do not soak up water. Water is better absorbed in wood chips for smoking. The good news… if you're ever camping, don't worry about rain soaking your fire wood!

the water only penetrated about 1/8 inch

## LACK OF OXYGEN CREATES SMOKE

This wood will catch fire as long as your smoker or grill is open. Once you close your lid and limit the oxygen inside the smoking chamber, the flames will extinguish and then the smoldering wood will start to billow wonderful, flavorful smoke. But be careful... no oxygen will snuff out your coals!

27

## TEMPERATURE ADVICE

### Controling The Heat When You Can't See The Vents?

Whether you have the grill cover on or off… it's just plain hard to see the bottom of the grill to know what kind of air flow you are getting from the vents. This is even more difficult if you have an ash bucket (which I recommend using because it speeds up cleaning). An ash bucket has a lever to control the air vents… which makes it impossible to tell where the vent cover vanes are over the air holes.

### Mark Your Openings!

I easily fixed this vent dilemma by using a marker and identifying the different vent openings. The thin line is when the vent is just barely cracked open, which just gives me enough air for a real slow smoke. The halfway mark gives me a little bit hotter smoking temperature. If I really need to crank up the heat, then I have a big "O" for where the vent is fully open. In the picture below, the vent is at the "O" which is fully open. Notice on my grill the 3 openings are located in one small area of the whole available space that you are able to move the lever back and forth… that's why I say it's so important to mark these 3 levels of openness.

## AIR VENT OPENINGS

**|** = Tiny Bit Open

**½** = Half Open

**O** = Fully Open

## WHEN IS THE MEAT DONE?

Any instant read thermometer is your best bet to get a quick temperature read on your meat. If you grill a lot, you can get pretty good at touching or poking your meat with your finger. The more tender your meat, the more rare it will be. Larger cuts of meat may require you to make a small cut—if the juices run clear, your meat is sufficiently done.

## RESTING YOUR MEAT

When you're done cooking, let your meat rest before slicing into it! Larger cuts of meats should rest a minimum of 10 to 20 minutes. When you take the meat off the grill, the outside temperature causes the heat to travel toward the center and continue to cook the meat. Resting allows the juices to be drawn inward. If you don't rest your meat, the juices will run out as soon as you slice into it.

## TEMPERATURE GUIDE

Here's a quick guideline for different meats and when they are done.

| | |
|---|---|
| **BEEF** | Rare: 120° to 130° |
| | Medium Rare: 130° to 135° |
| | Medium: 140° to 150° |
| | Medium Well: 155° to 165° |
| **PORK** | Medium: 140° |
| | Medium Well: 155° to 165° |
| **CHICKEN** | Breast: 160° to 165° |
| | Thigh: 170° to 175° |
| **FISH** | Medium Rare: 120° |
| | Medium: 135° |

# MY FAVORITE BBQ PARTY TOOLS

## CHARCOAL CHIMNEY

Chimneys are great for starting charcoal briquettes, so you can avoid the fuel taste of lighter fluid. I often have several chimneys going at different times, which gives me different timing options. Wad up newspapers to light the chimney; the design utilizes natural outdoor wind currents to get your coals glowing hot.

## WIRE GRILL BRUSH

The best wire brush for home use is Weber's® Triangle Grill Brush. It is sturdy, so you can use some good elbow grease when cleaning your grill. Forget those electric gadgets with little brushes that whirl around... they're a joke! Man-up and use a good sturdy brush that will withstand brute force when scrubbing your grill clean!

## LONG HANDLE TONGS

Make sure you have a good pair of tongs that fit in your hand and maintain a good grip. There are many tongs designed to look good, which are useless for flipping meats.

## BIG SPATULAS

The big spatula is amazing… there are times when you need to take a lot of food off a grill or smoker—and this spatula does the job quickly and efficiently. I absolutely love my big spatula! My favorite oversized spatula is made by Mr. Bar B Q®. Offset long blade spatulas work great for turning food that tongs can't handle (like fish) or scooping up tender veggies.

**Look how BIG my spatula is compared to the ruler!**

**Turn to page 33 to see how big this spatula really is!!**

## BASTING BRUSHES

Long handle brushes are best. Find soft bristles that won't ruin the surface of your meats or veggies. I like silicone basting brushes the best; they are soft and easy to clean.

## SAUCE MOP

For smaller basting and slathering… the silicone brush works just fine… but for big parties where I am grilling up a lot of ribs or chickens, I use a sauce mop. As a working Pitmaster, I love these mops because they hold a lot of sauce and I can slather a lot of ribs in a jiffy! However, these are not good for small jobs, as the mop head can soak up a whole cup of sauce just to get it primed. When your grill is smokin' hot, being able to work quickly is a must.

## SPRAYERS FOR FLAME CONTROL

Sometimes when you are cooking over a live fire or charcoal, your meat can catch on fire, especially if it is well marbled—or chicken with fat, rich skin. Keep a spray bottle handy in case your food starts flaring up too much. Since I do a lot of grilling, I have a portable lawn sprayer that I fill with water; it's a lot more efficient.

## INSTANT READ THERMOMETERS

Simple pocket meat thermometers are ok, but you could burn up your meats while waiting for the temperature to show up. Invest in a digital thermometer for instant readings. The best instant read thermometer is made by Thermapen Thermometer®. Insert the probe into the center of your meat and you will get an instant temperature reading. The quick flip-out probe makes it easy to use, instead of having to unravel a wire cord like on most temperature probes The best outdoor-to-indoor meat thermometer is Oregon Scientific. You can insert the wireless probe into your meat and put the digital reader inside your kitchen while you are prepping other foods. I love this!

**Instant Read Thermometer
by Thermapen Thermometer**

**Indoor/Outdoor Thermometer
by Oregon Scientific**

## MEAT INJECTORS

On large meats like turkey, Boston Pork Butts, or brisket, I like to inject the big muscles with marinades. You can marinade these big muscles by submerging them in a marinade for several days, however injectors work much faster. I also like meat injectors because you can inject flavorful marinades deep into the meat. For turkeys, I make a salty, chicken-flavored brine. For pork butts, I like a salty apple juice marinade. For briskets, I make a hearty beef au jus-flavored marinade. Sometimes, I add a good hot sauce to the marinade to give it some bite! Small meat marinade injectors can be found in grocery stores or big sporting good stores. Big meat injectors are easy to find on the Internet through barbecue enthusiasts' supplier websites. When I am preparing for a big barbecue party, the big injector makes fast work of injecting a smoker full of pork butts!

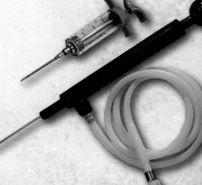

## WHICH SKEWERS ARE THE BEST?

CONFESSION! I am embarrassed to admit... the day we shot photos of the Chicken Satays and Beef Kabobs, I used round bamboo skewers for the satays *and* the kabobs. Normally, I would not use round skewers for kabobs. Let me explain... I like to use either a double steel kabob skewer, a flat single kabob skewer, or the flat bamboo skewers as pictured for kabobs. Using a round bamboo skewer can be difficult if your meat or veggies start spinning on you. The round skewer should only be used for satays, and the flat or double skewers for kabobs.

**Double Steel Kabob Skewer**

**Flat Single Kabob Skewer**

**Flat Bamboo Skewer**

**Round Bamboo Skewer**

## PROTECT SKEWERS WHEN GRILLING KABOBS

Keep your wooden skewers from burning up when making kabobs by folding several layers of aluminum foil and placing it under the skewer handles. It's also a good idea to concentrate your charcoal directly under the area where your kabobs will be grilled. This idea also works well on gas grills.

## WHIPPING CREAM DISPENSERS

No party is complete without a dessert that requires whipped cream! You can buy ready-made whipped cream in a can, but nothing beats the fresh dairy taste of real whipped cream. Ideally, I recommend using an electric mixer to beat fresh whipped cream. However, when time is running short, I recommend using the next best thing… a Whipping Cream Dispenser. These dispensers make beautiful, fluffy whipped cream without the use of stabilizers or preservatives. It's as simple as adding real heavy whipping cream, powdered sugar, and a few drops of real vanilla extract and inserting the $CO_2$ charger. Shake vigorously—and you'll have the most delicious, dairy fresh whipped cream!

31

## DISPOSABLE GLOVES

There are times, when fixing or preparing food, that it is better to wear thin disposable latex gloves. If at all possible, don't wear the white ones at a party!!! You don't want to look like you are ready to give someone a medical examination... go on-line and you can find a variety of colors. I personally like to wear black ones, but you may appreciate some other brighter colors; gals I have even seen them in pink!
Go on-line and search "colored disposable latex gloves."

## FIRE- AND HEAT-PROOF GLOVES

When you are working with live fire, hot coals, and hot foods... you want to have the right gloves handy to protect yourself. There are three types of gloves I use, depending on what I am doing. I have large, thick, insulated gloves for handling hot pans and getting close to intense hot heat when I am quick-grilling meats over live fire. I have a set of silicone red mitts for when I need to pick up a large piece of meat that is still very hot. Finally, I have silicone-lined gloves for light work where I need the flexibility of my fingers.

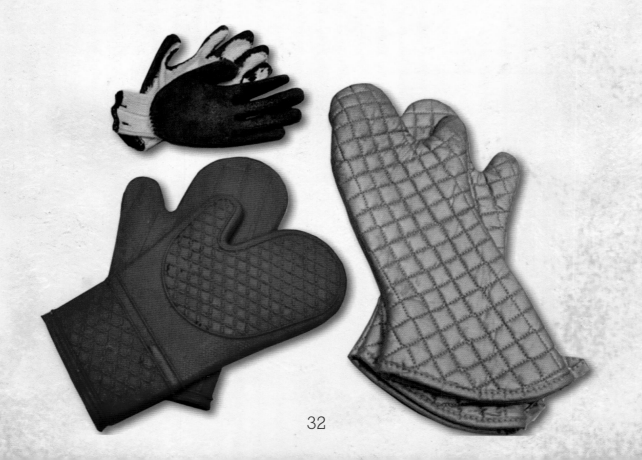

32

# My Grills & Smokers
## *...they are my heart and soul!*

For all the "inquiring minds" who always ask what kind of smokers I have at home… I love my grills and smokers and each one has its own specialities. Grills and smokers are to me like cars are to a racecar driver… or musical instruments to a musician. I couldn't live without them… they are my heart and soul. They greet me every time I walk by with their faint smoky aromas. I can't begin to tell you how many family and friends they have made indescribably happy by the wonderful barbecue they have provided! Also check out how big my spatula really is... I sure can remove a lot of food off a hot grill fast.

*Grill a man some food and he will eat for a day. Teach a man to grill and before you know it…*
*he'll have his whole backyard full of friends, drinking beer, and chowing down on his good-tasting barbecue;*
*and this is for the sole purpose of his needing to brag about his secret grilling recipes! ~Famous Dave*

# FAMOUS DAVE'S SMOKING TIPS

## What Kind Of Smoker Should I Buy?

For most weekend barbecue warriors just starting out, I recommend a good ol' black, charcoal-burning, Weber Kettle. You can grill on it and smoke in it. I also really like the Weber Kettle because you can add a rotisserie attachment to it; I absolutely love rotisserie smoked meats. One of the advantages of a rotisserie attachment is it bastes the meat in its own juices. There are some good electric smokers available, but I have always been a big fan of smoking over live smoldering coals. If you're deciding between a couple smokers, read a few blogs on the Internet; there are some very well-known barbecue pitmasters that explain in great detail the differences between all the best smokers.

## Grilling is Quick Work Over High Heat

There ain't nothing better than a juicy, grilled steak that's been flamed and lightly charred over an open fire. Hamburgers, hot dogs, brats, spicy charred chicken wings, marinated chicken breasts charred... they're all good grilled. But if you have the time, you'll enjoy how smoking can turn a rack of ribs into Hog Heaven, or a tough brisket into a juicy, tender as Mother's love, piece of beef. My all-time favorite is Cedar plank smoked Salmon with hints of maple syrup.

## If You Smoke...
## It's All About "Low and Slow"

Smoking isn't about speed—and how you prepare your meat is key to smoking success. I like to marinade my meats before seasoning and smoking. You can achieve amazing flavors by combining fresh fruit juices through marinating, spiciness through tasty rubs, and rich smoke through smoking. Smoking over low temperatures can take hours. Ribs can take anywhere from a couple of hours to 5 or 6 hours in the smoker. Larger cuts of meats like Boston Pork Butts or Beef Briskets can take up to 15 hours... but the results are worth it.

## The Fat Cap

On most big cuts of meat like Boston Pork Butts, Picnics, and Beef Brisket, there is a fat cap that can be thick. Don't cut off all the fat. The fat helps protect the meat during long hours of smoking, and as the fat renders it bastes the meat, keeping it nice and juicy. The fat cap is also what helps create the tasty "bark" that everyone craves.

*If it walks, flies, swims, moos, clucks, or oinks...*
*I can barbecue it!* ~Famous Dave

## Marinades, Rubs, Mops, and Sauces

One attribute of smoking is the craft of learning how to add tasty flavors to your meats. Marinades using fruit juices like apple juice and orange juice combined with spices and hot sauces are common. Adding vinegar helps break down the meat tissue, which also helps tenderize tough cuts of meat. Rubs are a closely guarded secret as they can have so many different nuances of flavors. A great rub is spicy, sweet, savory, and either a little bit hot or a whole lotta hot! ...all at the same time. A mop is used during the smoking process to keep the meat moist and build up the flavors of a great tasting bark. A great mop sauce may contain apple juice, vinegar, and hot sauce. Sauces generally are not used until the very end because adding a barbecue sauce too soon will cause the sugars in the sauce to burn. Most pitmasters will tell you that a sauce should not overpower the meat; the meat is the hero and it should be the center of attention—not the sauce.

## Should I Use a Water Bath?

Any heated box creates a dry, dry, dry environment, which will evaporate the natural juiciness of any meat and make it almost inedible. I recommend placing a pan of water directly over the heat source to provide some moistness in the smoker. Some cooks use beer, onions, or other herbs in the water bath... I do not because I feel these flavors interfere with the natural smoke flavors and give the meat an odd taste.

## Try Fruitwoods for Tasty Smoke Flavor!

Whether its fish, chicken, beef, pork, or even veggies... flavorful smoke adds a nice, rustic, outdoors flavor to food. Experiment with different hard woods like: oak, hickory, apple, cherry, pecan, maple, and mesquite, which all add a sweetness to the smoke. The fruit woods add a subtle, nice fruitiness to the meat. Hickory and apple wood are the most common woods used in smoking. Some people swear by mesquite. Mesquite burns really hot and fast; it is great for meats like steak... but for longer smokes the mesquite smoke is somewhat acrid. The only time I consider mesquite for smoking is for a brisket.

## Even Steven, Steady Eddie... Consistency is the Key

When you smoke meats, consistent, even temperature is the key to the perfect, tender smoked meat. There are scientific laws at work here, as there are temperature levels that need to be achieved for the meat to tenderize. If consistent temperatures are not achieved and the temperature fluctuates all over the place, the meat can turn tough. This is why it is so critical to watch the temperature; if the temperature goes too low, you can immediately add some charcoal. As a general rule, you need to add 10 briquettes every hour to maintain a constant temperature. Smoking over low temperatures for long hours achieves a nice smoky "bark." Bark is the dark, sticky, crunchy goodness that coats the meat and is naturally created by the meat and fat juices rising to the surface and caramelizing with the spices, sugar, and smoke.

## If You're Lookin'... You're Not Cookin'!

One of the common tendencies novice BBQ cooks have when smoking is the uncontrollable desire to constantly open up the smoker and look at the meat. Don't do this! Unless you are adding more charcoal to the smoldering coals... don't be tempted to always check your meat. The constant opening of the smoker fluctuates the temperatures too much.

## Flare-ups

One of the main reasons not to open your smoker/grill is to avoid flare-ups from the hot coals. When your meat is smoking over long periods of time, it drips fat into the bottom of your grill, which could flare up onto you or burn your meat. When you add wood chunks for smoke, a burst of fresh air could cause a flare-up onto you or your meat as well. When opening your smoker/grill (only to check on the meat or to add charcoal), have a squirt bottle or a cup of water handy to put out any flare-ups. You can also quickly put out a flame by placing the cover back on your grill and immediately closing all the vents. I have ruined many wonderful hunks of meat that caught on fire because I wasn't careful when opening up my smoker. You've been warned! Be careful when opening up a smoker that uses hot smoldering charcoal or wood.

## Temperature Control

One of the keys to a perfectly smoked piece of meat is temperature control. On smokers that utilize some type of computerized temperature controls this is easy. On smokers that use charcoal or open flames, you have to pay attention to the thermometer. The ideal smoking range generally is somewhere between 220 degrees and 275 degrees. Depending on the cook and the cooking style, some pitmasters like higher temperatures, but starting out I recommend 225 degrees for most meats. Regulate the temperature by opening and closing the vents. Don't close the vents too long or you'll put out your fire! On lids where the vent is off to one side, keep the bottom vents and the top vents opposite of each other open... this allows the smoke to travel across the smoker, and swirl around the meat before being drawn out of the smoker on the opposite end.

## Thin Blue Smoke, Billowing White Smoke, Black Smoke

Contrary to what you might think... big clouds of billowing white smoke are not always good. Too much smoke can cause a bitter acrid taste. The best smoke is a thin blue smoke. Soft smoke over time creates the best smoky flavor and enhances the flavors of the meat. Too much smoke will overpower the tastiness of the marinades and the natural goodness of the meat. Black Smoke is DANGER... it probably means you have a fire in your smoker and you are burning up your meat!

## When Is Your Meat Done?

Most smaller cuts of meat like ribs or pork tenderloin are done with an internal temperature of about 145 degrees. I like to finish ribs on a hot charcoal grill to caramelize the flavors. Chicken or any poultry is done with an internal temperature of about 165 degrees. If you have any question about the safety of your meat, then bringing up the temperature to 180 degrees is best. On big muscles that need to tenderize, smoking at low temperatures and achieving an internal temperature of 180 to 200 degrees will turn any tough meat tender, juicy, and tasty!

A perfect smoke ring!

## Smoke Ring

Often when folks get a smoked rib or chicken they notice a "redness" on the outside edge of the meat and wonder if the meat is undercooked. This pink color or redness is called a "Smoke Ring." This occurs when the natural juices of the meat combine with real smoke. A perfectly smoked meat will proudly display this outer edge smoke ring. This is a sign you are eating real barbecue done right!

When you take your time to slow smoke your meats slow & low over smoldering hardwoods, you won't dry your meats out. Look how juicy & tender this rib is after being smoked for 4 hours.

## Storing Your Smoked BBQ Meats

If your meats are done smoking and you're not ready to start serving your party, you will need to hold your meats somewhere and keep them warm without drying them out. I have found the best way to hold smoked meats is to wrap your pork butts, ribs, or briskets in heavy duty plastic wrap, covered with aluminum foil and then wrapped in a kitchen towel. Once wrapped, store your smoked meats in an ice cooler (minus the ice!); an ice cooler makes a nice insulated container to maintain the heat and smokiness. This frees up your oven for anything you have to do at the last minute for the party.

## Keep Notes!

I know, I know, you're probably thinking... UGH! All I want to do is smoke some meat, drink some beer, and have fun! Now you're telling me I need to take notes!?! YES. The key to smoking is figuring out what works for you and your smoker. Achieving great flavorful smoky foods is all about consistency. Once you understand how long you should marinade your meats, how much rub you should place on your meats and veggies, and how long you should smoke something... you will take all the guesswork out of great barbecuing and you'll enjoy more of the rewards of great-tasting barbecue. Best of all, you'll never have to worry about inviting guests over and finding out all the hard work you put into smoking your meat didn't turn out the way you thought it would.

DAVE SAYS...
FOLLOW THESE TIPS AND YOU'RE ON YOUR WAY TO BECOMING AN AWARD WINNING CHAMPION PITMASTER!

# FAMOUS DAVE'S

## *Legendary*

# APPETIZERS

### THE PASSION IS IN THE DETAILS

# EAT ★ LAUGH ★ PARTY

# TABLE OF CONTENTS

# BBQ Nachos Grande!

**"The World's Best BBQ Nachos"... seriously!** Here's a crowd-pleasing mountain of tastiness ~ crispy tortilla corn chips, BBQ baked beans, chili, BBQ pulled pork, jalapeños, black olives, lettuce, diced tomatoes, and drizzled with Famous Dave's BBQ Sauce and my spicy pumped-up sour cream. Get out of the way or you'll be trampled once your guests get a glimpse of this mouthwatering skyscraper of flavor!

# THIS BODACIOUS MOUNTAIN OF BBQ NACHOS WILL ABSOLUTELY MAKE YOU GO HOG WILD!

**Delightfully serves a party of 6**

**1 large bag of Mission Tri-Color Party Tortilla Chips**

**2 cups Dave's Party Time BBQ Baked Beans** (pg. 182)

**2 cups Tailgate Chili** (pg. 102)

**1 lb. BBQ pork, or brisket, or chicken… it's all good!**

**1/2 cup red onion, diced**

**1/2 cup pickled jalapeños, sliced**

**1/2 cup black olives, sliced**

**1/2 cup Roma tomatoes, diced** (I use these because they are not so fall-apart juicy)

**1 cup shredded sharp cheddar cheese**

**1 cup shredded lettuce**

## Drizzling Sauce One

**1/4 cup sour cream**

**1/2 tsp. Sriracha hot chili sauce**

**1 Tbsp. Famous Dave's BBQ Sauce**

## Drizzling Sauce Two

**1/4 cup Famous Dave's BBQ Sauce**

Clear off a large area on your table and line up all your ingredients. On the platter, start layering a foundation of tortilla chips. Then sprinkle the **BBQ Baked Beans** on top of the chips. Next, layer on some of the **Tailgate Chili**. Then spread the BBQ pork or your choice of BBQ meat evenly. Sprinkle the red onions, jalapeños, black olives, tomatoes, and cheese.

Repeat this layering until you have enough for one more layer. Then spread your lettuce over this big mountain. Spread the rest of the ingredients as a garnish over the lettuce.

For the First Drizzling Sauce, mix the sour cream, Sriracha hot chili sauce, and BBQ sauce and place in a squirt bottle. Drizzle over the nachos.

For the Second Drizzling Sauce, use Famous Dave's BBQ sauce in a squirt bottle and drizzle this artistically all over your masterpiece of deliciousness!

This towering mountain of flavor is why it's called BBQ Nachos Grande! Ole! You'll want to take a picture of this heap of goodness and you're going to be so proud of yourself, especially when everyone says "These are best tasting nachos ever!"

*"My doctor told me to stop having intimate dinners for four… unless there are three other people!"*
~Orson Welles

## Famous Dave's Hot Tips!

Start with a large ceramic platter so you have a good foundation for building a huge volcano of nachos. You know the saying… **Go Big or Go Home!** The bigger the better, I say. Besides, there isn't anything more impressive than a huge colorful display of scrumptious goodness piled high on a platter! You will need one large bag of restaurant-quality tortilla chips or God bless you if you want to make your own… it's always best to have the freshest quality ingredients and fresh tortilla chips have the perfect snap & crunch to them.

# GREAT BALLS OF FIRE!

**Come on baby light my fire!** These "Great Balls of Fire" are so flavorful they'll set your soul on fire and just spicy enough to make your tongue do the twist! When you taste these spicy nuggets of pure deliciousness… you'll never buy pre-made meatballs again. These flavor-packing meatballs also make incredible little burgers for the ultimate mini-sliders. This recipe also makes the best meatloaf on the planet. It's time to FIRE UP your meatballs!

**Delightfully serves a party of 8**

## MEATBALLS

3 lb. ground chuck

3 eggs, beaten

1/2 cup heavy whipping cream

2 cups Ritz cracker crumbs

1/2 cup sweet onion, finely diced

1/2 cup green bell pepper, finely diced

1/2 cup carrot, finely grated

1 tsp. salt

4 tsp. Famous Dave's Steak Seasoning (pg. 143)

1 Tbsp. Lea & Perrins Worcestershire Sauce NEW Thick Style

1 tsp. fresh ground black pepper

2 tsp. chili powder

1 Tbsp. prepared French's yellow mustard

2 Tbsp. Famous Dave's Rich & Sassy BBQ Sauce

Combine all ingredients for meatballs in a bowl. Mix thoroughly.

Use a small ice cream scoop to form meatballs. Dip the scoop in ice water as needed to keep the meatballs from sticking. Place meatballs on a sheet pan lined with baking parchment paper or aluminum foil. Bake at 350 degrees for 40 to 45 minutes. Makes about 48 - 1 1/2 ounce meatballs.

## APRICOT JALAPEÑO BBQ SAUCE

20 oz. Famous Dave's Rich & Sassy BBQ Sauce

12 oz. Smucker's Apricot Preserves

1/2 cup onion, finely diced

1/4 cup brined hot jalapeño peppers, finely diced

Combine sauce ingredients in a saucepan and heat over medium heat until vegetables are tender. Pour over meatballs and serve.

It's time to FIRE UP your meatballs!

Meatball Sliders

# SMOKIN' CHERRY BMBS

**I guess some things will never be like "The Good Old Days." One of my memories about growing up was my fascination with things that explode.** You can't get them anymore, but as a kid we were always delighted to get our hands on Cherry Bombs. Little, round red firecrackers with a green wick that exploded with a thunderous BOOM that could be heard all over the neighborhood.

These bacon-wrapped, whiskey-soaked, maraschino cherries and smoked hot Italian sausage explode with flavor and grilling makes them a great tasting barbecue appetizer. Soaking the cherries in a bourbon for a good week gives them the perfect flavor punch. The cooking process dissipates the alcohol, but the flavor stays and fuses perfectly with the cherries, bacon, and smoky sausage. I like serving these lil' tasties with my **Blackberry BBQ Sauce** (pg. 67). These Smokin' Cherry Bombs will go fast, so have plenty on hand!

## Delightfully serves a party!

**1 jar maraschino cherries**

**1 cup Jack Daniel's Tennessee Whiskey**

**1 lb. hot Italian sausages**

**1 lb. hickory smoked bacon**

**wire mesh for grill**

Drain the juice from the maraschino cherries container. Fill with Jack Daniel's; soak for at least 3 days.

Prepare your grill. Par-grill Italian sausages so they are not entirely raw; they will finish cooking when wrapped with bacon on the grill. Depending on the size of your bacon, cut bacon strips into thirds or halves. Cut sausages into 1/2-inch slices.

Assemble your cherry bombs. Take a sausage slice, place a cherry on top, then wrap with bacon, and use a toothpick to secure.

Place Cherry Bombs on a wire mesh and place on grill (see photo). Grill until the bacon is crisp. As the Cherry Bombs cook, fat will fall into the grill and may cause flare-ups. You don't want your appetizers catching on fire, so having them on a wire mesh makes it easy to lift them off the grill quickly so you can douse the flames.

Serve with **Blackberry BBQ Sauce (**pg. 67).

45

# HOG Dog Fritters & Cajun Mustard

**OINK ME if these ain't the best appetizers you've ever tasted. These are some real "Pigs Gone Wild!"** Smoky sausages bundled in corn fritters and served with a fantastic spicy Cajun Mustard. These bundles of happiness are so amazing I honestly haven't figured out how to make them fast enough because friends devour them as fast as I can make them. These are serious adult corn dogs, but your kids will love them too!

## Delightfully serves a party of 5 or 6

1/2 cup cornmeal

1/2 cup stone-ground cornmeal

1/2 cup flour

1/2 cup Jiffy Yellow Cake Mix

1 tsp. salt

1/4 tsp. cayenne

2 tsp. baking powder

1 egg

2 Tbsp. sugar

1 cup whole milk

2 Tbsp. melted butter

1 can (15 oz.) sweet corn, drained

2 lb smoked sausages cut into 1" cubes

1/4 cup additional flour for coating the sausage

peanut oil for deep frying

In a large bowl, combine cornmeals, 1/2 cup flour, cake mix, salt, cayenne, and baking powder. Set aside.

In a separate bowl, whisk egg and sugar until sugar is dissolved. Add milk and combine. Add the milk mixture, sweet corn, and melted butter to the dry ingredients bowl; mix well. Cover bowl with plastic wrap and let the batter rest in the refrigerator for 30 minutes.

Heat peanut oil in a deep fryer over medium heat to 375 degrees. Remove batter from refrigerator and set out. In a small bowl, place 1/4 cup flour. Roll sausage in flour and then place into the corn bread batter. Using a large oiled spoon, swirl the sausage in the batter to coat well. Using your wrist, give the spoon a swirl so the batter wraps around the sausage as you place the battered sausage into the hot oil. This takes practice, but it's the key to keeping your sausage wrapped evenly in the batter while it gets dipped into the oil. Be careful not to cause splashes. Deep fry until a beautiful golden brown. Serve with **Cajun Mustard.**

## Cajun Mustard

1/2 cup yellow mustard

2 Tbsp. Grandma's Original Unsulphured Molasses

2 Tbsp. Louisiana Hot Sauce

In a small dish, mix ingredients well.

These *HOG Dogs* are so tasty
your party animals will be begging
for more... so go ahead and make
enough for a whole block party!

47

**PUBLIC SERVICE ANNOUNCEMENT:**
Every day thousands of innocent plants are massively slaughtered by vegetarians. Help end this senseless violence. **EAT BACON!**

48

# SMOKIN' DRAGONS!

## MONSTER Stuffed Jalapeños

**Smokin' Dragons are sure to get sparks shooting from your head!**
Over-sized jalapeños, stuffed with BBQ pork or BBQ chicken and spiced-up cream cheese, wrapped in hickory-smoked bacon, and a secret surprise in each one! These Smokin' Dragons are guaranteed to ignite the fire within but in a good way… they're spicy, crunchy, and creamy good. Your guests will wonder what's so flavorful and buried under the veggie cream cheese… it's dried cherries! The **Black Raspberry Dipping Sauce** is to die for. These stuffed flavor bombs are wickedly addicting, so make sure you have plenty on hand.

---

### Delightfully serves a party of 8

**1/2 lb. of BBQ pulled pork or BBQ meat of your choice**

**12 fresh BIG jalapeños**
(the curved ones have more heat)

**2 Tbsp. Knorr Dry Vegetable Soup Mix**

**8 oz. cream cheese, softened**

**1 package dried cherries**

**2 lb. thin hickory bacon**
(the thin stuff wraps better)

First get your charcoal grill going with an aluminum package of wrapped chunks of hickory wood to smoke your jalapeños. Next, smoke your choice of BBQ meat or you can go to any Famous Dave's and order a pound of BBQ brisket, chopped pork, or pulled chicken. "You can always find BBQ meat products at your local grocer if you don't have a Famous Dave's or the time to smoke up a pork butt or a chicken yourself."

I use the biggest jalapeños I can find, which take almost a full slice of bacon. If you get smaller jalapeños, you may only need half a slice of bacon per pepper. When you're working with this many jalapeños… I want to caution you about touching yourself anywhere sensitive (you know what I mean) or you'll be screaming to high heaven! I highly suggest you wear protective gloves. Cut jalapeños into halves, remove seeds, core, and lay flat on a tray and set aside.

Empty the dry soup mix into a resealable plastic bag and crush the dry mix. Then, in a medium bowl, add 2 tablespoons of the crushed soup mix to the cream cheese; mix well.

Assemble your jalapeños. First, line the bottom of the jalapeño peppers with dried cherries. Then put a spoonful of cream cheese on top of the cherries. Finally, layer the BBQ meat on top of the cream cheese and wrap the entire jalapeño with bacon. Use a toothpick to secure if needed.

Place the stuffed jalapeño in the smoker until bacon turns crispy. Serve with **Black Raspberry Dipping Sauce**. The taste of jalapeños wrapped in bacon smoked over a charcoal fire is absolutely amazing! But (sigh) yes, you can make these in your oven.

## BLACK RASPBERRY DIPPING SAUCE

**10 oz. frozen raspberries in sugar juice**

**8 oz. cream cheese, softened**

**4 oz. sour cream**

**1/4 cup Dickenson Black Raspberry Preserves**

**2 tsp. Sriracha hot chili sauce**

**1/2 tsp. crushed red pepper flakes**

Thaw frozen raspberries. In a bowl, thoroughly mix cream cheese, sour cream, black raspberry preserves, Sriracha hot chili sauce, and crushed red pepper flakes. Add the thawed raspberries and mix well. Refrigerate until use.

# Lip-Smackin' Dang Good Wings!

**There's one thing everyone can agree on... Lip-Smackin' Dang Good Wings are one of the most popular fan favorite appetizers for any party, game day, or barbeque.** Forget all the hassles of deep frying... throwing these wings on the grill gives them a whole new smoky dimension in tastiness and crunch! Dress them in my **Robust Honey Teriyaki Sauce**, **Original Hot Buffalo**, and **NEW Orange Chipotle BBQ Sauce**. AND you're going to love my **Cool Blues Cheese Dip** (pg. 52)... wings never tasted so good!

Orange Chipotle Wings

Hot Buffalo Wings

Cool Blues Cheese Dip

Honey Teriyaki Wings

*LIP-SMACKIN'...*

## Delightfully serves a party of 6

**36 Wings**

**3 Tbsp. Knorr Chicken Base-Sam's Club Brand or Maggi Chicken Soup Brand**

**3 Tbsp. salt**

**2 Tbsp. lemon pepper**

**2 Tbsp. sweet paprika**

**2 Tbsp. granulated garlic**

**2 Tbsp. granulated onion**

**1 Tbsp. ground celery seed**

**1 Tbsp. fresh ground black pepper**

**2 tsp. cayenne**

**1 tsp. Accent (optional)**

**3/4 cup pure water**

**1/4 cup light olive oil or canola oil**

In a small bowl, mix all the dry ingredients. Next, slowly add water while stirring to avoid clumping. It's important this mixture is completely mixed before adding oil. Add olive oil last and mix well.

Lightly rub wings with seasoning mix. Place wings in a large plastic container or resealable plastic bag and marinate in the refrigerator at least 4 hours or overnight.

Prepare charcoal grill with hickory wood. Wipe off excess seasoning before grilling. Grill until internal temperature is 180 degrees and juices run clear. The skin should be nicely charred and wings should easily pull apart. If you struggle to pull the wings apart, then they should cook a little longer.

Toss grilled wings in one of my wing sauces (or serve them naked!). Serve with my **Cool Blues Cheese Dip** (pg. 52)!

---

## Orange Chipotle BBQ Sauce

**1 1/2 cups Famous Dave's Rich & Sassy BBQ Sauce**

**1/2 cup orange juice concentrate**

**1/2 cup orange marmalade**

**1 tsp. Sriracha hot chili sauce**

**2 tsp. chipotle peppers in adobo sauce**

Mix ingredients together and toss with 12 grilled wings.

---

## Dave's Own Original Hot Buffalo Wing Sauce (Medium Hot)

**1/4 lb. butter**

**2 cups Frank's Red Hot Sauce**

**2 Tbsp. Sriracha hot chili sauce**

**1/4 tsp. cayenne pepper**

**1/4 cup blue agave honey**

In a sauce pan, melt butter. Add all ingredients into melted butter and mix well. Toss with 12 grilled wings.

If a milder sauce is preferred… use 1 Tbsp. of Sriracha and eliminate cayenne pepper.

## Robust Honey Teriyaki Sauce

**1/4 cup teriyaki sauce**

**1/2 cup dark brown sugar**

**1/4 cup clover honey**

**2 Tbsp. fresh ginger, finely grated**

**1 Tbsp. fresh garlic, finely minced and crushed**

**1/4 cup fresh lime juice**

**1/4 cup Mizkan Nakano Original Seasoned Rice Vinegar**

**1 Tbsp. Sambal Oelek Chili Paste**

**1 Tbsp. Sriracha hot chili sauce**

**1 tsp. sesame seed oil**

**2 Tbsp. cornstarch**

**1 cup Famous Dave's Sweet & Zesty BBQ Sauce**

**Toasted sesame seeds for garnish**

Mix all ingredients EXCEPT cornstarch and Famous Dave's BBQ Sauce together in a sauce pan over medium-high heat.

Mix in cornstarch and bring to a boil. Boil for one minute and remove pan from heat. Stir in Famous Dave's Sweet & Zesty BBQ Sauce.

Toss with 12 grilled wings and garnish with toasted sesame seeds.

If a milder sauce is desired… reduce the amount of Sriracha and Sambal Oelek accordingly.

# COOL BLUES CHEESE DIP

**If you love wings and great tasting robust salads with explosions of flavor… you're going to love this blue cheese dressing & dip.** I like using Gorgonzola, because it has a more robust flavor—perfect for creating this amazing blue cheese dressing & dip. Get the wings smokin'… the lettuce flying … turn up the butt rockin' blues and get to partying, I say!

## Delightfully serves a party of 8

1 cup mayonnaise

4 oz. packet dry ranch dressing mix

1/4 cup buttermilk

1 cup sour cream

8 oz. cream cheese, softened

1/4 tsp. salt

1/4 tsp. fresh ground black pepper

1/4 tsp. cayenne

1/4 cup Parmesan Reggiano Cheese

1/2 cup Gorgonzola crumbles

Don't even think of using the parmesan cheese in the green container! What makes this blue cheese dressing so flavorful is the robustness of real cheeses… so get the best cheeses and ingredients as possible.

Mix all ingredients except Gorgonzola together in a food processor or using a whip smash; add Gorgonzola and whip vigorously to blend the cheese into the dressing. Don't over blend, you still want a fair amount of cheese chunks. Chill, covered, until serving time or overnight to allow the flavors to marry.

**Yields:** approximately 4 cups.

52

"I cook with wine.
Sometimes I even
add it to the food!"
~ W.C. Fields

53

Pictures from Famous Dave's BBQ & Blues Club
Minneapolis, MN

# Fired-Up! Chicken BBQ Quesadilla

**OLÉ!!! Your party guests are going to love these Fired-Up! Chicken BBQ Quesadillas stuffed with flavor!** I make these quesadillas with pita bread rather than flour tortillas, which have a tendency to tear. I like the pita bread because it provides a firmer foundation for this hand-held party sandwich and the toasty, buttered, grilled pita adds great flavor to the sandwich. This quesadilla is lip-smacking tasty—especially once the flavorful rotisserie chicken gets squashed between the fresh crunchy veggies and the robust cheeses… it's a South of the Border Party for the mouth!

**Delightfully serves a party of 5**

1 large sweet onion

1/2 stick butter

1 Rotisserie Chicken, hand shredded

10 pita bread slices

Butter Flavored Pam Non-Stick Spray

2 cups sharp cheddar cheese, shredded

2 cups Queso Fresco Mexican Style Farmer's Cheese, shredded

1 bottle Famous Dave's Texas Pit BBQ Sauce

---

# BBQ PICO DE GALLO

2 ears of sweet corn, grilled and niblets sheared off

3 Roma tomatoes, diced

1 green bell pepper, diced

1 jalapeño, seeded and finely minced

2 limes, juiced

2 Tbsp. Famous Dave's Texas Pit BBQ Sauce

couple of sprigs of cilantro, rough chopped

In bowl, place grilled corn niblets, diced Roma tomatoes, green bell pepper, minced jalapeño, lime juice, and BBQ Sauce. Toss to mix and refrigerate. Can be made a day ahead of party. Garnish with cilantro before serving.

Make the **BBQ Pico de Gallo** and refrigerate.

The caramelized onions are optional... fresh sliced onions can be used. In a sauté pan, melt butter and caramelize onions; set aside.

Either rotisserie a chicken yourself or buy a rotisserie chicken from the grocery store. Remove skin and the meat from the bones. Pull and chunk chicken meat by hand and place meat in a bowl. It's important to have all your ingredients, including the BBQ Pico de Gallo, assembled on a tray next to your grill to have available to immediately make each quesadilla as soon as the pita comes off the grill while the cheese is still hot.

Using two pita slices at a time, spray Pam on one of each slice… this side will go down on the grill. Next, place shredded Queso Fresco Cheese on one pita slice and on the other pita place the shredded cheddar cheese. Grill to melt cheese. Once cheese begins to melt, remove immediately from grill.

Now start assembling the quesadillas. On the Queso Fresco cheese pita, place shredded chicken and drizzle with BBQ Sauce. Top with BBQ Pico De Gallo. Lastly, top with the caramelized onion. Place the other cheddar cheese pita bread on top, press down firmly with your hand to firm up the sandwich. The melted cheese will hold the pita together. Slice into three sections. Repeat this process with remaining pitas and ingredients. Serve with your choice of dressing or BBQ sauce.

**Yields:** 15 quesadillas.

IT'S A SOUTH OF THE BORDER PARTY FOR THE MOUTH!

# Festive Party Guacamole

**It doesn't have to be Cinco de Mayo for you to enjoy this great tasting Festive Party Guacamole.** What makes party food festive is the creativity of taking a recipe and embellishing it with gusto; guacamole is the perfect recipe to test your creativity! Everyone likes unexpected surprises that spice things up. This recipe features pineapple and Grand Marnier but you can add bacon, sun-dried tomatoes, Serrano peppers, thyme, basil, cumin, shallots, grilled cherry tomatoes, grilled corn, mangos, bananas, grapefruit, fire-roasted salsa, blue cheese, dried cranberries, lump crab, lobster, tequila, Cointreau... well, you get the picture.

---

### Delightfully serves a party of 4

**1 cup fresh pineapple, drained and diced**

**1 large garlic clove, finely minced**

**1-1/2 tsp. kosher salt**

**4 avocados**

**2 Tbsp. fresh lime juice**

**1-1/2 tsp. Aleppo chili pepper**

**1/4 tsp. fresh ground black pepper**

**2 Tbsp. fresh cilantro, finely minced**

**1/2 cup red onion, diced**

**1 jalapeño, seeded and finely minced**

**2 Roma tomatoes, diced**

**2 Tbsp. Grand Marnier**

Dice pineapple first, let pineapple drain after dicing.

In a bowl, combine garlic clove and salt. Gently muddle this with the back of a spoon to bruise and blend flavors. Lightly mash avocados to desired chunkiness and combine with lime juice, which will help the avocado from turning brown. Add the Aleppo chili pepper, black pepper, cilantro, onion, and jalapeño. Mix well.

Add tomatoes, pineapple, and Grand Marnier last to keep them from being decimated while you mash and mix everything else. Mix gently.

Cover with plastic wrap. Push plastic wrap directly into the guacamole to keep air from turning the dip brown. Refrigerate until ready to use.

## Famous Dave's Hot Tips!

Jalapeño peppers can be bland and not spicy hot, so for more heat I leave the seeds and dice them up along with the pepper. The seeds will always spice things up guaranteed!

Aleppo chili pepper is found at Penzey's Spice Stores or you can order it online. It has a wonderful chili taste without tasting like a bowl of chili. And yes, if you absolutely can't find the time to order the Aleppo pepper... you can substitute with chili powder.

# The Best Guacamole Recipe EVER!

# BBQ Smoky Porkies

**It just ain't a party without these BBQ Smoky Porkies!** These aren't the usual itty bitty "cocktail weenies!" I really haven't found a good little cocktail weenie that didn't taste like rubber. These BBQ Smoky Porkies are made with full-sized Johnsonville Smoked Sausages and then stuffed with my Famous Dave's Spicy Pickles and Sharp Cheddar Cheese. MMmmmm… Delicious!

### Delightfully serves a party of 8

**2 lb. Johnsonville Smoked Sausages**

**1 jar of Famous Dave's Spicy Pickle Spears**

**1/2 lb. block of sharp cheddar cheese**

**1 package hickory smoked bacon**

Preheat charcoal grill. Slice the smoked sausages in half and with a sharp paring knife cut a square slot into the sausage half to hold the pickle spear and cheese.

Place pickle spear alongside a thin slice of cheese and place into the sausage. Wrap with bacon, secure with toothpick if needed.

Grill on indirect heat till bacon crisps. Place the porkies around the edge of the glowing coals, but not directly over the charcoal. "You don't want to put these directly over the hot coals as the fat from the bacon will quickly create a blazing fire."

Serve with **Drunken Apricot BBQ Sauce** for dipping.

## Drunken Apricot BBQ Sauce

**10 oz. Famous Dave's Sweet & Zesty BBQ Sauce**

**10 oz. Famous Dave's Rich & Sassy BBQ Sauce**

**10 oz. apricot preserves**

**1 shot glass of Kahlua** (optional)

In a medium-size bowl, gently mix the sauces together with the apricot preserves and Kahlua.

## Famous Dave's Hot Tips!

Find a specialty sausage like chorizo, andouille, or chicken & wild rice sausage that will give your party guests an unexpected surprise! Try different cheeses for stuffing the sausages. You can even use different veggies or fruits to stuff alongside the cheese like apricots or dates… the key is to have fun and not get stuck doing the same thing every time! Whatever you do… don't be tempted to buy those bags stuffed with all the little cocktail weenies… they are boring!

# PIGGY-LICIOUS!

# BBQ Chicken Satay & Peanut Satay Sauce

**No party would be complete without some kind of meat skewered and set on fire!** There are many Asian peanut sauce recipes, but mine is... sooo good you'll swear you were standing in front of a Hong Kong street vendor firing up these tasty treats while you wait. Chop Chop!

## Delightfully serves a party of 8

**6 chicken breasts pounded flat and sliced lengthwise** (You should get 3+ strips per breast.)

**24 skewers soaked in water**

## Peanut Satay Sauce

**1 cup Smart Balance Rich Roast Creamy Peanut Butter**

**1-1/2 cup Mitsukan Seasoned Rice Vinegar**

**1/4 cup Kame Hoisin Sauce**

**1/4 cup Famous Dave's BBQ Sauce**

**1/2 cup Kikkoman Soy Sauce**

**1/2 cup Asian Sweet Chili Sauce, plus extra for drizzling**

**1/3 cup sugar**

**2 tsp. sesame seed oil**

**1-1/2 tsp. fresh ginger, finely grated**

**1/2 tsp. crushed red peppers**

This is a three-day recipe. On the first day, make the Peanut Satay Sauce. In a large bowl, mix the sauce ingredients together. Cover and refrigerate overnight. You need to let the peanut sauce set so all the flavors can get acquainted!

On the second day, prepare the chicken. Divide the sauce; put 1/3 in a big plastic bag, and put the other 2/3 sauce in an airtight container and refrigerate.

Place the chicken in the big plastic bag with the peanut sauce. Marinate at least 4 hours or overnight.

On the third day, weave the chicken on skewers and grill 5 minutes on each side. Serve with remaining 2/3 sauce for dipping. Once the skewers are done, I like to drizzle the skewers with Asian Sweet Chili sauce; it complements the Peanut Satay Sauce very nicely.

**Yields:** approximately 20 skewers.

*These tasty chicken satays are flame kissed and flavor spanked!*

# TEXAS BUCKAROO BBQ SALSA

**If this isn't your first rodeo…you're going to do the two-step after you taste this delightfully spicy Texas Buckaroo BBQ Salsa.** It's fresh, spicy, and crunchy, but more than anything its color will brighten up your party table. This BBQ Salsa is a flavorful topping for crunchy tortilla chips or toasted pita bread. Warm it up and you have a great side dish. This BBQ Salsa is a terrific and versatile party recipe!

**Delightfully Serves a Party of 6 to 8**

**1 can** (15 oz.) **Bush's Baked Beans**

**1 can** (15 oz.) **black beans**

**1 can** (11 oz.) **sweet corn niblets**

**1 cup red onion, diced**

**1 cup green bell pepper, diced**

**1 cup red bell pepper, diced**

**3 Roma tomatoes, diced**

**1/4 cup  balsamic vinegar**

**1/2 cup Famous Dave's Rich & Sassy BBQ Sauce**

**1 Tbsp. Frank's Hot Sauce**

**1/4 cup light olive oil**

**2 garlic cloves, minced & mashed**

**1 tsp. kosher salt**

**1/4 tsp. fresh ground black pepper to taste**

**2 avocados, chopped**

**1/2  cup  scallions, thinly sliced on a bias**

**1/3  cup  fresh cilantro, rough chopped** (optional)

**1/4 cup sour cream**

**1 Tbsp. BBQ sauce**

**1/4 tsp. cayenne pepper**

**1 bag restaurant style tortilla chips or make your own**

## Famous Dave's Hot Tips!

This tasty ensemble of veggies and beans is a great recipe to keep in your refrigerator for a delightful anytime snack. Don't wait for a party to enjoy this robust BBQ salsa!

In a large bowl, place a large colander. First, empty the baked beans into the colander and let drain. Next, empty the black beans and sweet corn niblets into the colander using their juices to wash off the baked bean juices. After draining, remove the colander and put beans in a large bowl. Discard juices. Add red onions, red and green bell peppers, and tomatoes,.

In a small bowl, add balsamic vinegar, BBQ sauce, hot sauce, olive oil, minced garlic, salt and pepper. Mix well. Refrigerate and let mixture marinate for several hours before serving.

I like to add the avocados last so they don't get mushed up. Fold avocados into the salsa and gently mix all ingredients together. Garnish with scallions and cilantro.

Mix sour cream with BBQ sauce and cayenne; place in a plastic baggie. Snip off one corner of the baggie and drizzle over the salsa.

Serve with tortilla chips.

# Smoked Baby Red Stuffers

**These delightful fully-loaded little baby red potatoes are just as fabulous as their big over-stuffed cousins.** You're going to love these baby reds stuffed with smoky potato, hickory smoked bacon, and tasty cheeses! But it's the roasted walnuts that are the delightful tasty treat inside that will have your guests scrambling for more!

**Delightfully serves a party of 6**

12 small baby reds or white-skinned baby potatoes

1/2 cup cooked hickory-smoked bacon, divided

1/4 cup + 2 Tbsp. butter

1/3 cup walnuts, toasted

1/2 cup heavy whipping cream

1/4 cup cream cheese

1/4 cup parmesan cheese

1 tsp. kosher salt

1/4 tsp. fresh ground black pepper

1/2 cup pepper jack cheese

1/2 cup sharp cheddar cheese

dash of paprika

1/4 cup chives, finely chopped

Prepare your grill with charcoal and a couple of chunks of hickory wrapped in aluminum foil. Your grill should be about 350° and smoking. Place baby red potatoes on grill grate and they should be smoked/baked in about 30 minutes.

Cook bacon till crispy. Once bacon cools, chop into small pieces.

In a sauté pan, melt 2 Tbsp. butter and toast walnuts. Once the walnuts are a nice golden brown, immediately take the pan off the heat and empty the walnuts into a metal bowl. This will stop the hot butter from burning the walnuts.

Check to see if the baby reds are done by sticking a small, sharp knife in through the top to test the tenderness. You want your potatoes tender, so the knife can easily be inserted. Do NOT overcook the potatoes or they will collapse when hollowed out. Once the potatoes have cooled, slice 1/3 of the top off the potato. Scoop out the insides and reserve.

In a sauce pan, heat the heavy cream and butter. When it almost simmers, turn down the heat; slowly add the cream cheese and parmesan cheese, mixing thoroughly. Remove from heat. Take the tops and the scooped out insides of the potatoes and mash into the heavy cream cheese mixture. Add salt, pepper, half the bacon, and the walnuts.

Stuff potato shells with a heaping amount of the filling and arrange potatoes on an aluminum foil-covered or parchment lined baking sheet. Generously sprinkle the pepper jack and cheddar cheese on top of the filled potatoes. Next, lightly sprinkle with bacon and paprika. Place back on the grill or in the oven to "quick melt" the cheeses. Garnish with finely chopped chives.

## Famous Dave's Hot Tips!

I always smoke a couple large russets—just in case I need more mashed potatoes for stuffing.

# Blackberry Tenderloin Crostinis

**Blackberry Pork Tenderloin Crostinis are the perfect make-ahead appetizer to make entertaining a snap!** All the ingredients can be prepared ahead of time and then assembled right before your guests arrive. The rich combination of smoky pork tenderloin, drizzled with a delicious blackberry BBQ sauce, sprinkled with creamy goat cheese crumbles, and a hint of fresh mint… will impress your guests. These amazing Blackberry Tenderloin Crostinis saved our butts in the Food Network's $50,000 "Best In Smoke" Challenge in 2011.

**Delightfully serves a party of 20**

4 pork tenderloins

All-Purpose Pork Marinade

Jimmie's Old Southern Pork Butt Rub
(pg. 132)

2 French baguettes

olive oil

8 oz. goat cheese crumbles

2 bunches fresh mint

Black Raspberry BBQ Sauce

Prepare my **All Purpose Pork Marinade** and marinade pork tenderloins for 4 hours. Prepare charcoal grill with hickory or apple wood. After 4 hours, remove tenderloins from marinade and discard marinade.

Prepare **Jimmie's Old Southern Pork Butt Rub** (pg. 132). Lightly sprinkle loins with rub. Smoke over indirect heat for about 45 minutes or until internal temperature reaches 145 degrees. Remove loins and cover lightly with aluminum foil. Let loins rest until cool. Prepare **Blackberry BBQ Sauce**.

Slice French baguettes thin to less than a 1/2 inch. Baste with olive oil and grill to a nice golden brown. Thinly slice smoked pork tenderloins on a bias. Next, take the pork rub, place into a coffee grinder, and grind into a fine dust. Place in a salt shaker and very lightly dust sliced meat. Layer pork on toast. Spoon Blackberry BBQ Sauce over the pork and top with goat cheese.

Pick the leaves off a sprig of mint. Roll leaves up and thinly slice. Sprinkle mint over the goat cheese. Don't overdo it with the mint… a hint of mint goes a long way.

**Yields:** 40 appetizers, or 2 per person.

## All-Purpose Pork Marinade

2 cups apple juice

1/2 cup apple juice concentrate

3 Tbsp. Frank's Hot Sauce

1 Tbsp. salt

1 tsp. Accent (optional)

Mix ingredients together and store in an airtight container or plastic bag until ready to marinate.

## Blackberry BBQ Sauce

1/2 cup apple juice concentrate

1/4 cup blue agave honey

2 pints blackberries

10 oz. Dickinson's Seedless Black Raspberry Preserves

20 oz. bottle Famous Dave's Sweet & Zesty BBQ Sauce

In a saucepan, mix apple juice concentrate with blue agave honey and heat up. Once the juice bubbles, add the blackberries. Simmer over medium heat until blackberries start to dissolve and mixture thickens to the consistency of a heavy syrup. Add Dickenson's Black Raspberry Seedless Preserves and Famous Dave's Sweet & Zesty BBQ Sauce to the pan. Bring to a simmer and remove pan from heat.

# Spinach Artichoke Stuffed Mushroom Caps

**These little stuffed mushroom caps will put the wang-dang-doodle back into your party!** I've had people tell me they hate mushrooms until they tasted these little, decadent, tasty delights. The stuffing recipe also doubles as a rich, creamy, and flavorful Spinach Artichoke Dip that you can spread on buttery toast points as well. Guaranteed to be a party favorite!

**Delightfully serves a party of 12**

5 oz. frozen spinach

24 crimini or large button mushroom caps 1-1/2 to 2 inches wide

8 oz. cream cheese, softened

2 Tbsp. Famous Dave's BBQ Sauce

1 cup Hellman's Mayonnaise

2 Tbsp. Knorr Vegetable Soup Dry Mix (crush before use)

1 cup parmesan cheese, grated, divided

1/2 cup Asiago cheese, grated

1/3 cup sun-dried tomatoes in oil, drained, finely diced

4 oz. artichoke hearts, drained, rough chopped

1/2 tsp. crushed red pepper flakes

1/2 cup sharp cheddar cheese, grated

2 Tbsp. parsley, minced

Thaw spinach, chop, squeeze dry, and set aside.

Remove the stems and inside gills from mushrooms, wash and pat dry. Slice a very thin slice off the "bottom" of the mushrooms so they stand up straight.

In a large bowl, combine cream cheese, BBQ sauce, and mayonnaise. Add soup mix. Mix well. Add 1/2 cup parmesan cheese, Asiago cheese, spinach, sun-dried tomatoes, artichoke hearts, and red pepper flakes, and mix well. Refrigerate at least 2 hours.

Fill mushrooms with dip and sprinkle remaining parmesan cheese and cheddar cheese over top of the stuffed mushrooms. Place under a broiler to quickly melt cheese.

*CAUTION:* You are "quick melting" the cheese. If you get the mushrooms too hot they will wilt and fall apart. Garnish with parsley.

**Yields:** 2 dozen mushrooms.

**OINK IF YOU LOVE BBQ!**

## Famous Dave's Hot Tips!

I usually put the Knorr dry soup mix in a bowl and crush the dried veggies a bit and mix them well with the rest of the soup mix before I use it.

# Smoked Salmon Paté Cucumber Cups

**This is my favorite smoked salmon paté served up in crisp, cold cucumber cups.** These are fun appetizers and the robust smoky salmon makes for a very tasty quick bite and colorful plate presentation. This recipe is the best-tasting way to use smoky salmon as an appetizer!

## Delightfully serves a party of 12

1 can (15 oz.) **red salmon, drained**

8 oz. **cream cheese, softened**

2 Tbsp. **Famous Dave's BBQ Sauce**

2 tsp. **fresh lemon juice**

1 tsp. **prepared horseradish**

1 tsp. **Worcestershire sauce**

1/2 tsp. **kosher salt**

1/4 tsp. **white pepper**

1/4 tsp. **Wright's Liquid Smoke**

1 Tbsp. **sweet onion, finely minced**

1 Tbsp. **fresh jalapeño, seeded, finely minced**

2 Tbsp. **sun-dried tomato, finely minced**

1 Tbsp. **Knorr's Dry Vegetable Soup Mix** (crushed & mixed)

2 large **cucumbers**

**Garnish: chives, parsley, black olives... anything fun and colorful!**

· Remove skin and bones from salmon, and flake.

In a blender, combine cream cheese, BBQ sauce, lemon juice, horseradish, Worcestershire, salt, white pepper and liquid smoke. Process until smooth, and place in a bowl.

Next, combine the cream cheese mixture, salmon, onion, jalapeño, sun-dried tomatoes, and dry soup mix; mix well. Refrigerate until ready to use.

Wash cucumbers and create stripes by peeling strips on skin. Slice cucumbers into 1-1/4 inch thick rounds. Using a melon baller, scoop out the interior and some of the sides—leaving at least 1/4-inch thick bottom. Wet a paper towel and place on a plate. Put prepped cucumber cups upside down on the plate in-between wet paper towels. Fit the plate into a large Ziploc® bag and refrigerate till you're ready to serve, up to 24 hours.

Fill cucumber cups just before your party begins; the salmon tasts better chilled and the refrigerated cucumber cups create a nice, cold, crisp holder for the salmon paté. To make sure your guests love you, keep these chilled in the refrigerator after filling and before serving.

**Yields:** 24 cucumber cups or 2 servings per person.

*There is nothing more exhilarating than to have friends, neighbors, and even strangers tell you that your party was the best ever... and the food was nothing short of being mouthwatering, scrumptiously delicious! Great-tasting food requires complete attention to how tasty you make your food look. Create thrilling, visual feasts of "eye candy"... people eat with their eyes first!*

# BBQ PARTY IN A GLASS!

## Individual 9-Layer BBQ Party Dip

**If you ever served a layered dip, you'll know how popular they are for parties. While these layered dips start out looking fabulous…they quickly start to look like a messy, muddy football field after a few swipes from hungry guests.** My Individual 9-Layer BBQ Party Dip will be a real winner at your next party; your guests will love being able to grab & go with these personal-sized servings. AND you'll never have to worry about double dippers! This dip features the robust barbecue flavors of smoky BBQ chicken, BBQ baked beans, a seasoned cream cheese, **Festive Party Guacamole** (pg. 56), sharp cheddar cheese, jalapeños, cherry tomatoes, and black olives making it colorful, tasty, and delicious!

**Delightfully serves a party of 8**

8 plastic cocktail glasses

1 bag tortilla chips, restaurant quality

1 smoky rotisserie BBQ chicken*

1 can (16 oz.) BBQ baked beans, drained

1/4 cup Famous Dave's BBQ Sauce

16 oz. cream cheese, softened

1 packet Knorr Vegetable Recipe Dry Mix (crushed & mixed)

Festive Party Guacamole (pg. 56)

2 cups shredded sharp cheddar cheese

1 cup brined HOT or fresh jalapeños (to taste)

2 cups cherry tomatoes, halved

1-1/2 cups sliced black olives

cilantro

* you can substitute with 1 pound of BBQ pork or brisket.

Prepare the seasoned cream by combining cream cheese and dry vegetable packet. Mix well and let set at least 2 hours before using.

In a clear plastic cocktail glass, layer the following ingredients:

**First Layer:** smoky rotisserie BBQ chicken, about 2 ounces of meat per glass.

**Second Layer:** BBQ baked beans

**Third Layer:** thin drizzle of Famous Dave's BBQ Sauce

**Fourth Layer:** seasoned cream cheese

**Fifth Layer: Festive Party Guacamole** (pg. 56)

**Sixth Layer:** shredded sharp cheddar cheese

**Seventh Layer:** brined HOT or fresh jalapeños (to taste)

**Eighth Layer:** halved cherry tomatoes

**Ninth Layer:** sliced black olives

Garnish with a tortilla chip and cilantro

# BBQ Deviled Eggs

**These party favorites are just downright tasty!** In fact, they're so devilishly tasty... they're heavenly! Enjoy these delicious BBQ Deviled Eggs without feeling guilty about your diet. Eggs are healthy and nutritious. So go ahead and eat a bunch of these little devils!

---

**Delightfully serves a party of 12**

12  large eggs

4 oz. cream cheese, softened

1/4  cup  Hellman's Mayonnaise

1 Tbsp. yellow mustard

1 Tbsp. Knorr's Dry Vegetable Soup Mix (crushed & mixed)

1/4 cup Famous Dave's Spicy Pickles, minced

2 Tbsp. Famous Dave's BBQ Sauce

1/4  tsp.  white pepper

1/4 tsp.  Louisiana Hot Sauce

dash paprika

**Garnishes - Be creative and have fun!**

Pierce a small hole in the large end of each egg to center the yolk with a sewing needle. Place the eggs in a large saucepan. Add enough cold water to cover. Bring to a boil. Remove from heat and cover. Let stand for 20 minutes; drain. Add cold water to cover. Repeat the draining and covering with cold water process several times or until the eggs are cool. Knock the eggs together under running water to loosen the eggs from the shells. Discard shells.

Cut the eggs in half lengthwise. Remove the yolks and rinse egg whites if necessary. Arrange the egg whites on a serving platter. Mash the egg yolks in a bowl. Add the cream cheese, mayonnaise, mustard, and dry soup mix. Next, add pickles, BBQ sauce, pepper, and hot sauce and mix well. Fill egg white halves with mixture. Sprinkle with paprika and garnish.

Garnish: paprika, chives, avocados, pimento strips, black olives, sweet pickles... "It's a party so be fun and festive with your garnishes, you're guests will love your little surprises!"

Chill, covered, until serving time.

**Yields:** 24 servings.

# Lil' Sweet Potato Babies

**These are a delightful mini rendition of a big sweet potato, but they are the perfect tasty appetizer for any barbeque bash.** I know you're probably saying, "I've never seen a mini-sweet potato." Yes, and that's true, but these are made with mini red potatoes and stuffed with mashed sweet potatoes... they work perfectly together. Your family and friends will get a kick out of these delicious Lil' Sweet Potato Babies.

---

**Delightfully serves a party of 8**

**8 mini red potatoes**

**1 can** (15 oz.) **sweet potatoes or yams in syrup**

**2 Tbsp. brown sugar**

**1 tsp. cinnamon**

**2 Tbsp. melted butter**

**1 bag mini marshmallows**

*When life gives you lemons... just squeeze some into sweet tea and thank the Lord you were born Southern!*

*-Jimmie Anderson, Dave's Dad*

Wash mini red potatoes. Boil for 10 minutes to get slightly tender. Drain and cool.

Heat oven to 300 degrees. Slice off top 1/3 of potato. Using a melon baller, scoop out the centers of the potatoes and reserve. You will get about 1 cup of potato. Drain and measure out 1 cup of yams. In a bowl, add reserved potato and yams; mash to a pulp. Add brown sugar and cinnamon, mix into potatoes. Add melted butter, mash and mix well.

Fill hollowed out potato shells with sweet yam mixture... leaving stuffing slightly mounded. Top with mini marshmallows. Spray pan with non-stick cooking spray. Bake 10 to 15 minutes until mini-marshmallows turn golden brown.

This recipe makes 8 individual potatoes, but they're small enough where folks may not be able to stop at one!

Good Eatin' At BB's

Sandwiches WITH HOME CUT FRIES

Memphis Wings

Southern Fried Catfish B.B.'s FAVORITE

# CATFISH LIPS!

## A Spicy Cajun Appetizer

Laissez les bons temps rouler... "Let the good times roll!" **If you love fish with a lot of flavor... then you'll be whistlin' Dixie with this spicy catfish appetizer.** These Catfish Lips make a great party appetizer or the perfect picnic finger food. Catfish is a great hearty fish that doesn't fall apart when you slice it into finger-size strips. Today, catfish are raised in clear freshwater farms so they don't have a muddy taste. Whenever I make these catfish fingers, folks are beggin' for the recipe. This recipe is also great for a good old-fashion fish fry... just leave the fillets whole.

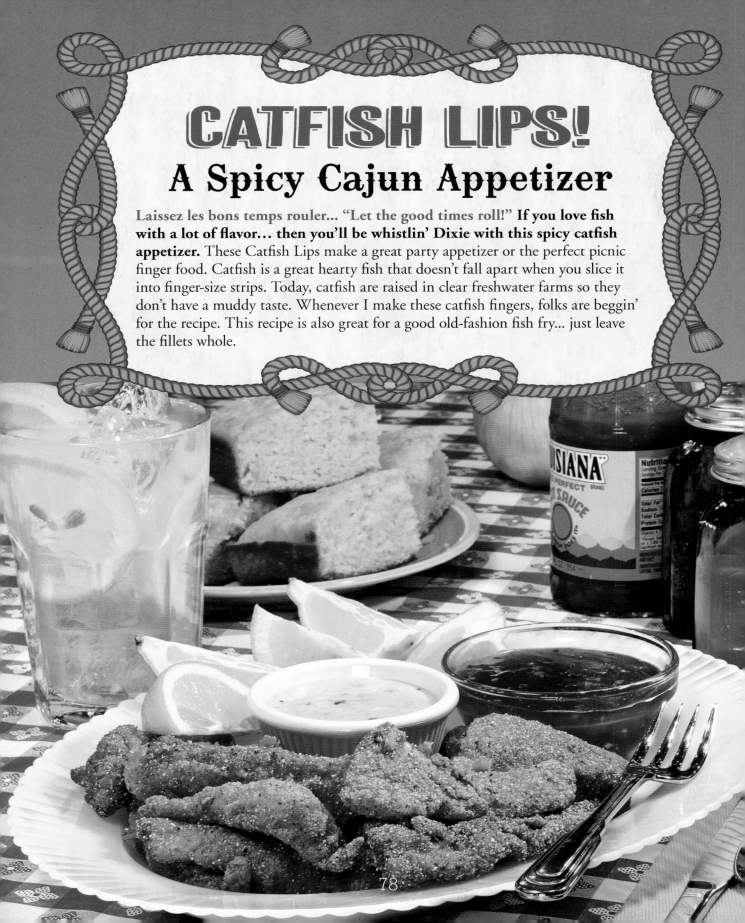

# CATFISH LIPS!

**Delightfully serves a party of 6**

6 catfish fillets

2 cups buttermilk

3 cans (12oz. size) Carnation Evaporated Milk

2 Tbsp. Louisiana Hot Sauce

2-1/4 cups cornmeal

1-1/4 cups yellow corn flour*

4 Tbsp. salt

3 Tbsp. lemon pepper

2 Tbsp. granulated garlic powder

1 Tbsp. onion powder

1 Tbsp. paprika

1 Tbsp. Accent (optional)

2 tsp. fresh ground black pepper

1 tsp. cayenne pepper

peanut oil or vegetable shortening for frying

lemon wedges

Cut catfish into strips approximately 1" wide x 4" long. You can usually get about 5 or 6 strips per fillet. In a large, plastic container with a lid, place buttermilk, evaporated milk, and hot sauce. Mix well; add catfish. Marinate in the refrigerator at least 2 hours.

Mix cornmeal, corn flour, and seasonings together in a shallow bowl. Dredge catfish fingers into cornmeal bread, Deep fry in hot oil until the fingers are a deep golden brown. Serve with lemon wedges and dipping sauces.

*There are a number of small specialty mills like Bob's Red Mill or Hodgson Mill that make "corn flour," which is different from "cornmeal." Usually you can find corn flour in your local specialty grocer.

---

# JALAPEÑO SWEET & SOUR DIPPING SAUCE

10 oz. jar sweet & sour sauce

3 Tbsp. sweet chili sauce

1 Tbsp. brined hot jalapeño slices, finely minced

Mix ingredients together and serve in a small dipping bowl.

# CAJUN TARTAR SAUCE

1 cup Hellmann's Mayonnaise

1 Tbsp. stone-ground mustard

1/2 cup Famous Dave's Spicy Pickle Relish

1/4 cup sweet onion, finely diced

1 Tbsp. Louisiana Hot Sauce

Mix ingredients together and serve in a small dipping bowl.

*Embarrassing story—*

*My dad was born in Idabel, Oklahoma... right smack in the middle of the Bible-belt, so growing up when I was told how Jesus fed the multitudes... it was always catfish and cornbread! You can imagine the howling laughter from my Sunday school classmates when I tried to correct the Sunday school teacher!!!*

*~ Famous Dave Anderson*

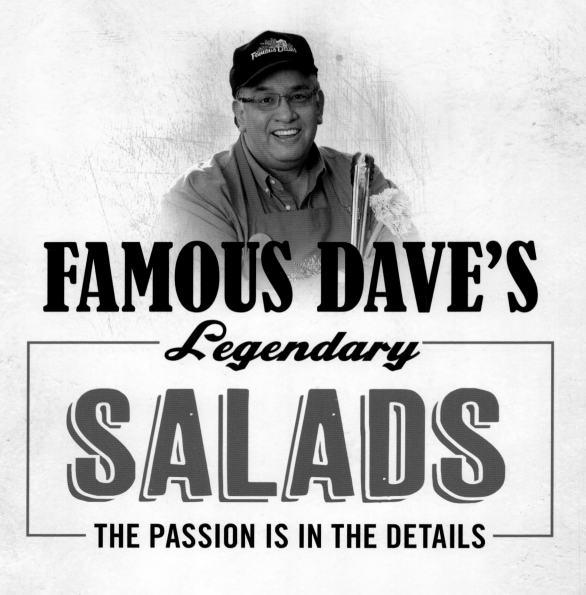

# FAMOUS DAVE'S
## *Legendary*
# SALADS
### THE PASSION IS IN THE DETAILS

EAT ★ LAUGH ★ PARTY

# TABLE OF CONTENTS

# Fruit Salsa Dip & Cinnamon Chips

**Yummy, Yummy, Yummy!** This is a fun, simple, fruit dip served with toasty cinnamon chips. It's light and fresh, but here's the what makes this fun…serve it in a carved watermelon… it's the perfect way to get the party started. Very kid friendly!

---

**Delightfully serves a party of 12**

1 personal-sized watermelon, carved

2 cups watermelon, cubed

1/4 cup water

1 Tbsp. lemon juice

2 Golden Delicious apples

12 oz. Dannon vanilla yogurt

6 oz. Kraft Creamy Poppy Seed Dressing

3 Tbsp. apricot preserves

1 lb. strawberries, sliced

8 oz. raspberries

8 oz. blueberries

8 oz. green seedless grapes, sliced in half

1 cup mandarin oranges, drained

1/4 cup sugar

1 Tbsp. cinnamon

10 - 10-inch flour tortillas

butter-flavored cooking spray

Wash fruit. Carve watermelon; scoop out in big pieces, then cube into bite-size pieces. In a bowl, pour water and lemon juice. Peel, core, and chop apples and place in lemon water.

Mix vanilla yogurt, poppy seed dressing, and apricot preserves. Gently toss strawberries, raspberries, blueberries, grapes, apples, and mandarin oranges in the dressing. Cover and chill in the refrigerator at least 2 hours.

Preheat oven to 350 degrees. Mix sugar and cinnamon together. Cut flour tortillas into six wedges. Spray with butter spray and sprinkle cinnamon sugar over the tortillas. Bake chips until they start turning brown and crisp, and the cinnamon sugar starts bubbling. Upon removing from oven sprinkle the chips with another dusting of cinnamon sugar. Cool chips.

Cover watermelon with plastic wrap and refrigerate overnight. Place fruit salsa in a fun carved watermelon and serve with cinnamon chips.

This recipe is best when held overnight.

SMILE... YOU'RE THE PARTY!

# Potato Salad Party!

**Don't dump nondescript mounds of white potato salad into bowls!** Jumpstart the fun with this killer mustardy, bacon potato salad by garnishing the glasses like a Bloody Mary. Serve with a celery stick and a stacked garnish of olives, pickles, and cherry tomatoes and rim the glass with honey dipped in tasty Southwestern lemon pepper spice. Go ahead and pimp out your potato salad… add some bling and all your side dishes will look like they're ready to party!

---

## Delightfully serves a party of 12

3 lbs. Yukon gold potatoes

1-1/4 cup mayonnaise

1/2 cup sour cream

3 Tbsp. yellow mustard

2 tsp. dry mustard

1/3 cup Famous Dave's BBQ Sauce

1 cup Famous Dave's Spicy Pickle Juice

1 Tbsp. kosher salt

1/2 tsp. white pepper

1/4 tsp. cayenne pepper

1/2 cup sweet yellow onion, minced

1/2 cup celery, finely sliced

1/2 cup Famous Dave's Spicy Pickles, finely diced

4 hard boiled eggs, finely diced

1/4 cup pimentos, chopped

1/2 cup cooked hickory smoked bacon, chopped

### Rim of Glass Spice

1/4 cup simple syrup

1/2 cup Famous Dave's Rib Rub

1/4 cup lemon pepper

1/4 cup Baker's Fine Sugar

Start your charcoal grill with a small amount of charcoal. Once hot, add an aluminum foil pouch with a few large hickory or oak chunks wrapped inside.

Place potatoes in a large pot and cover with water. Add a couple teaspoons of kosher salt to the water and bring to a boil over high heat. Once boiling, reduce heat and simmer for 15 minutes or until potatoes become tender. Drain and cool in an ice bath until you can handle and remove skins. By this time, your grill and the chunks of wood should be smoking up a storm. Quarter potatoes and place on grill grate. Smoke for about 5 minutes. Remove and let cool. Dice into small chunks.

In a large bowl, add mayo, sour cream, yellow mustard, dry mustard, BBQ sauce, pickle juice, kosher salt, white pepper, and cayenne pepper, and mix well. Next, add onion, celery, spicy pickles, diced eggs, pimentos, and bacon. Add potatoes to salad dressing ingredients to blend well. Best if held overnight.

Place simple syrup in a shallow dish. In a second shallow dish, combine Rib Rub, lemon pepper, and sugar. Take serving cups and dip the rim in simple syrup and then into rib rub mixture. Fill each glass with potato salad and store in refrigerator until serving.

Garnish with leafy celery hearts and cherry tomatoes, sweet gherkin, olive, and cherry tomato speared on a big cocktail swizzle stick…or create your own fun festive garnish!

## Famous Dave's Hot Tips!

Don't depend on your local store for disposable plastic party cups. Go online and you'll find a wealth of really fun disposable, decorative plastic party cups and fun serving dishes! Planning ahead and finding interesting ways to decorate your table adds a lifetime of fond memories to your party… plus everyone will gossip about you being the party hostess with the mostess!

This recipe serves 12 portions at 6.5 ounces each; this makes a big difference on the serving size of your party cups. You can actually serve more people by pre-proportioning your food, instead of setting out a mounded bowl of potato salad.

*Kick start summer's barbecue season with these tasty salads!*

# BBQ CHOPPED CHICKEN SALAD

**Throw away the fork and get yourself a spoon…cuz you're gonna want to dig in and shovel this stuff up to your mouth!** I like this salad because it is packed with flavor and all the crispy ingredients are chopped into tasty bite-sized pieces. There's no right or wrong way to make this salad… whatever makes you happy… toss it into this salad. My tasty BBQ salad dressing combined with the smoky chicken is what makes this salad a standout compared to all other chopped salads. This BBQ Chopped Salad is a fun way to start your barbecue party—or an entire meal by itself.

**Delightfully serves a party of 6**

1 head iceberg lettuce

2 heads romaine lettuce

1 apple, cored and diced

2 tsp. Ball Fruit-Fresh® Produce Protector

1 lb. smoked bacon, crumbled

2 cans (3.5 oz. size) **sliced black olives**

3 - 7 oz. grilled chicken breasts, diced

4 hard boiled eggs, chopped

1/4 cup sunflower seeds

1 pint cherry tomatoes, halved

1 cucumber, diced

1 can (11 oz.) **corn niblets, drained\***

4 oz. goat cheese crumbles

1/2 cup green onions, sliced thin on a bias

## BBQ CHOPPED SALAD DRESSING

1 cup mayonnaise

1/2 cup Western dressing

1/2 cup Famous Dave's Rich & Sassy BBQ Sauce

1 cup buttermilk

1 package (2.5 oz.) **Ranch dressing dry mix**

1/4 tsp. fresh fine ground black pepper

1/2 cup blue cheese crumbles

This salad is traditionally made by throwing all the ingredients together, and then using two big knives, you start chopping away until all the ingredients are bite-sized. I prefer to prep each ingredient separately…it just seems to work better without all the mess chopping everything together makes. Although it can be a royal pain, I would encourage you to hand-tear the lettuce into bite-sized pieces instead of using knives. Hand shredded lettuce looks more "home style" than seeing lettuce squared off.

Prepare **BBQ Chopped Salad Dressing** in advance. Core & dice apple; hold in a bowl of ice water with 2 teaspoons of Ball Fruit Fresh Protector. Prepare the other ingredients.

Using a big bowl, mix all ingredients together and toss with BBQ Chopped Salad Dressing.

Serve immediately on a cold serving plate.

**\*Use 2 cups of fresh sweet corn if possible.**

Mix the first 6 ingredients together and place in a blender.

Add blue cheese crumbles and turn on blender. Blend until smooth. Refrigerate and hold 2 hours until needed; best if held overnight.

This is a great-tasting salad dressing you'll want to use on other salads. Keep some handy in the refrigerator!

## Famous Dave's Hot Tips!

Crispness is your goal with a chopped salad. When all your ingredients are chopped small, they lose their crispness faster. When I prep this salad, as soon as I have one ingredient chopped, I cover it immediately with plastic wrap and place it into the refrigerator until I am ready to combine all the ingredients. This helps maintain freshness and crispness. A cold, crisp chopped salad is a joy to eat!

# CHERRY WALNUT PASTA SALAD

**You're going to love the crunchiness, freshness, and tastiness of this delicious all-around party pasta salad.** Almost a meal in itself, this Cherry Walnut Pasta Salad is a terrific side dish, one all your guests will love. This type of salad also travels well... bring it to your next big shindig!

## Delightfully serves a party of 6

1 box fusilli macaroni

1 cup hickory smoked bacon (optional)

1 cup walnuts, toasted and chopped

1 cup mayonnaise

1/4 cup orange juice concentrate

2 Tbsp. white balsamic vinegar

1 tsp. kosher salt

1/4 tsp. black pepper

1/2 tsp. paprika

1/2 cup dried cherries

1 cup cherry tomatoes, sliced

1 cup seedless green grapes, halved

1 cup celery, chopped

1/2 cup sweet onion, diced

1 lb. fresh green beans, ends trimmed, cut in half

Prepare pasta according to directions. Cook bacon, rough chop, and set aside. Preheat oven to 350 degrees. Place walnuts on a baking sheet and bake until lightly roasted—about 10 minutes.

In a medium bowl, combine mayonnaise with orange juice concentrate, balsamic vinegar, salt, pepper, and paprika. Add cooked pasta to mayonnaise mixture and mix well.

Add dried cherries, cherry tomatoes, green grapes, celery, onion, walnuts, green beans, and bacon; mix well.

Cover and refrigerate at least 2 hours before serving.

# Tropical Paradise Salad

**Summer's the right time for Jimmy Buffet songs, the fresh taste of the islands, and a fun barbecue party on the beach.** This tropically inspired salad is a fun, colorful mix of mangoes, fresh pineapple, kiwi fruit, star fruit, mandarin oranges, and strawberries topped with a Poppy Seed Raspberry Vinaigrette.

ARRIVED

TROPICAL PARADISE

no. 4 12 1961

**Delightfully serves a beach party of 6**

**6 cups romaine lettuce, hand-torn**

**6 cups spring lettuce**

**1 fresh pineapple, cored and sliced into bite-sized pieces**

**2 cups mandarin oranges**

**2 pints strawberries, sliced**

**2 mangoes, cut into strips**

**4 kiwi fruit, rind removed and sliced**

**3 star fruit, sliced**

**1 cup slivered almonds**

For this salad, you have to build each salad individually on the plates get the right presentation.

Mix lettuces and place two cups on each plate. Prepare all the fruit, and individually place on the salads. This salad requires a little finesse in placing the fruit so that you create a WOW impression.

Garnish with slivered almonds and serve with **Poppy Seed Raspberry Vinaigrette Dressing** on the side.

## Poppy Seed Raspberry Vinaigrette Dressing

**When you are throwing a party, you just don't have time to make everything from scratch.** There are just so many good dressings on the market that mixing your two favorites creates an amazing and unique salad dressing without any hassle!

**1 bottle - poppy seed dressing**

**1 bottle - raspberry vinaigrette dressing**

Buy your favorite poppy seed dressing and raspberry vinaigrette dressing and mix the bottles 50/50. Shake and store until ready to serve.

# Strawberry Spinach Salad

**This salad is simple and delicious.** Your guests will enjoy the combination of flavors from the tangy Feta cheese, toasty candied walnuts, fresh strawberries, and robust raspberry vinaigrette… this salad is delightfully cool and refreshing on a hot summer day!

## Delightfully serves a party of 6

1 large garlic clove, minced in a garlic press

2 tsp. blue agave honey

2 tsp. stone-ground mustard

1 cup fresh raspberries, mashed

3 Tbsp. white balsamic vinegar

2 Tbsp. light brown sugar

1/2 cup light olive oil

6 cups springtime baby lettuce

6 cups baby spinach

1 pint fresh strawberries

1 cup crumbled Feta cheese

1 cup Trader Joe's Candied Walnuts

Prepare dressing by combining garlic, agave honey, mustard, mashed raspberries, balsamic vinegar, brown sugar, and oil. Whisk vigorously.

Mix baby lettuces with baby spinach; add strawberries, and feta cheese. Toss with dressing, plate, and garnish with candied walnuts.

# AVOCADO POTATO SALAD

**If you love the buttery smooth taste of avocados…
you're gonna love this incredibly flavorful potato salad!**
Yumminess Heaven… Avocado Potato Salad. This will
be your new favorite potato salad, it's that good!

## Delightfully serves a party of 12

3 lb. baby red potatoes, boiled until tender

1 cup mayonnaise

3 tsp. Ball Fruit-Fresh Produce Protector

2 cups cherry tomatoes, sliced

1 cup red onion, diced

2 tsp. kosher salt

2 tsp. Aleppo chili pepper

1/4 tsp. black pepper

1 Tbsp. flat Italian parsley, minced

5 large avocados

Pick baby red potatoes that are all about the same size. Wash and place in pot; fill with water until there is about 1 inch covering the potatoes. Add two teaspoons of salt and bring water to a boil over high heat. Once boiling, reduce heat and continue simmering for 12 minutes or until potatoes are tender. Drain and cool in an ice bath. Do not remove skins. Cut potatoes into bite-sized chunks and set aside.

In a large bowl, mix the mayonnaise with the Ball Fruit-Fresh Produce Protector and mix well. Add tomatoes, onions, salt, chili pepper, black pepper, and parsley, then combine.

Core avocados, remove the meat of the avocado and rough chop. Mix avocados into the mayonnaise mixture. Add in potatoes. Using a heavy spoon, mix everything together with the purpose of mashing up some of the avocados to blend everything into the mayo mixture. Garnish with parsley. If you're not going to serve it right away, cover by placing a plastic film directly over the salad.

93

# The Farmer's Market Salad
## A Garden Medley of Freshness!

**My Best-Tasting Salad EVER!** My famous Farmer's Market Salad is so delicious anytime of the year. I like this salad because it is so light, crispy, crunchy, fresh, and full of flavor… you'd think the farmer's daughter walked right from her garden into the kitchen, tossed everything together, and set this medley of tasty freshness right in front of you. The Cranberry Raspberry Balsamic Vinaigrette is perfectly light and sweet enough to complement all the other ingredients. When I serve this salad, everyone's plate is licked clean as a whistle and they are hounding me for the recipe!

**Delightfully serves a party of 8**

**Marinade** *(Optional ~ this salad is very good without meat!)*

**4- 6 oz. chicken breasts**

**Wish Bone Robust Italian Dressing**

**1 cup orange juice**

**Famous Dave's Steak Seasoning** (pg. 143)

**Salad**

**8 cold plates** (this is necessary for a great-tasting, crisp salad!)

**8 oz. Mesclun lettuce\***

**8 oz. Romaine lettuce, hand torn**

**8 oz. cherry tomatoes, sliced** (6 tomatoes per salad)

**4 oz. walnuts, chopped** (1/2 oz. per salad\*\*)

**8 oz. dried Cranberries** (1 oz. per salad)

**4 oz. crumbled goat cheese** (1/2 oz. per salad)

**2 large sweet & tasty apples or two large pears**

**2 cup cold water**

**1 Tbsp. lemon juice**

**Cranberry Raspberry Balsamic Vinaigrette** (pg. 96)

\*Mesclun lettuce is a mixed assortment of young salad leaves, which might include: baby green romaine, green leaf lettuce, radicchio or Italian spinach, arugula, Swiss Chard, dandelion, baby spinach, etc.

\*\*Don't be tempted to sugar your walnuts. Sometimes on a salad, I like to caramelize sugar on my nuts ;o) … but for this salad the extra sweetness of candied nuts is not necessary. What you are really looking for is just a simple crunchiness for texture.

## ZESTY ALL-PURPOSE CHICKEN MARINADE

Prepare Zesty All-Purpose Chicken Marinade (Optional ~ salad is also very good without meat.) Take a bottle of Wish Bone Robust Italian Dressing and DO NOT SHAKE. Squeeze bottle over a sink and remove top oil. Oil in marinade is not helpful and you can prove this just by tasting the oil that you are squeezing out of the dressing (there is no taste to the oil). After you remove the oil, pour dressing into a resealable plastic bag. Add orange juice and chicken breasts. Refrigerate at least 4 hours; best overnight.

Remove chicken breasts from marinade and discard marinade. Wipe chicken breasts clean of marinade and season with **Famous Dave's Steak Seasoning** (pg. 143).

Cook on a char grill until done; make sure you get some nice grill marks on the chicken. The chicken can be served warm on the salad, or refrigerated and served cold if you want the chicken done in advance of your party.

## THE FARMER'S MARKET SALAD

Tear chicken breasts into bite-size chunks and divide into 8 portions. You will need about 3 ounces of chicken meat per salad. You can use a knife, but then the chicken has that "processed" look… tearing makes the salad look "down home!"

Next, core and quarter apples. Slice thin, about 8 to 10 slices per quartered apple. Cut apple slices in half. You will use about 1 to 2 ounces of slices per salad. Place sliced apples in 2 cups of water with lemon juice until you are ready to build salad.

Hand-tear Romaine lettuce (don't even think of chopping with a knife!) and mix with Mesclun greens. You will use 2 ounces of greens per plate. Toss with half of the **Cranberry Raspberry Balsamic Vinaigrette** (pg. 96).

To build the salad, take a cold plate and place a handful of salad greens on the plate and start adding half of the apples, cherry tomato slices, dried cranberries, walnuts, and chicken. Add another handful of salad on top and then add the remaining cherry tomato slices, apples, dried cranberries, chicken, and walnuts. Top with crumbled goat cheese and sprinkle evenly. With the remaining vinaigrette… drizzle a tablespoon over the salad.

*You may be thinking… just 2 ounces of lettuce greens? Check out the picture on the right, 2 ounces of baby lettuces is a lot of greens, perfect enough for a great-tasting salad!*

# CRANBERRY RASPBERRY BALSAMIC VINAIGRETTE

**1 cup apple juice**

**1/4 cup apple juice concentrate**

**2 Tbsp. cranberry raspberry fruit juice concentrate**

**2 Tbsp. quality balsamic vinegar**

**1 Tbsp. Dijon mustard**

**1/4 tsp. Louisiana Hot Sauce** (couple of dashes)

**1/4 cup light olive oil**

Mix apple juice, apple concentrate, cranberry raspberry fruit juice concentrate, balsamic vinegar, Dijon mustard, and hot sauce, and place in a blender. Turn on blender, slowly drizzle olive oil into the blender in a fine stream. This will emulsify the dressing so it doesn't separate so fast.

Rihanna Miles, the best summer helper ever!

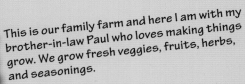

This is our family farm and here I am with my brother-in-law Paul who loves making things grow. We grow fresh veggies, fruits, herbs, and seasonings.

*Somebody told me that eating greens would help get you skinny. I said, "What? Are you kidding me? Have you ever seen cows? Greens are all they eat and they're fat!"*

~Famous Dave Anderson

# FAMOUS DAVE'S

## *Legendary*

# SOUPS & SANDWICHES

## THE PASSION IS IN THE DETAILS

# EAT ★ LAUGH ★ PARTY

# TABLE OF CONTENTS

While the original recipe generally calls for lima beans… I use fresh string beans because kids will eat this stew—but not with lima beans.

Add the chicken last so it doesn't shred and look stringy when served. When you add the chicken, be careful not to "vigorously stir" the stew. Instead "swirl" the chicken so it stays in chunks.

*"Brunswick Stew is what happens when small mammals carrying ears of corn fall into barbeque pits!"*

# A BARBECUE CLASSIC... Put Some Soul in Your Bowl!
# "Get Elected" Brunswick Stew

**If you want to get elected... this is the perfect block party or tailgating soup!** Brunswick stew is a true Southern American classic soup, dating back to the late 1800s from Brunswick, Georgia. It's a hunter's stew, and originally boasted of squirrels and any available vegetables that could be tossed into a big black kettle... so there is no exact recipe. This is a true backyard-barbecue-type of stew where it bubbles away all day and just keeps getting better and better! The smoky meats make this stew a real, full-flavored, hearty meal to be enjoyed with a backyard full of friends! If you're running for office, this Brunswick stew is sure to get you elected...

---

## Delightfully serves a party of 8

1 can (10.5 oz.) **Campbell's Beef Consommé**

3 lbs. **chicken, smoked and boned, shredded into chunks by hand**

1 lb. **sausage, chopped, charred & twice smoked sliced into 1/4-inch rounds** (all beef kielbasa or andouille sausage work well)

1 cup **hickory-smoked bacon**

2 Tbsp. **bacon grease**

1 cup **sweet onions, chopped**

1 cup **celery, chopped**

1 fresh **jalapeño pepper, NOT seeded, finely minced**

2 large **garlic cloves, finely minced and smashed**

1 cup **green bell pepper, chopped**

2 cups **Progresso Chicken Stock or rich homemade stock**

1 lb. **potatoes, diced**

1 can (28 oz.) **whole peeled Roma tomatoes, crushed and chopped**

1/2 cup **Famous Dave's Rich & Sassy BBQ Sauce**

2 Tbsp. **Lea & Perrins New Thick Style Worcestershire Sauce**

1 tsp. **kosher salt** (to taste)

1/2 tsp. **fresh ground black pepper**

1/4 tsp. **cayenne pepper**

1 lb. **smoked beef brisket, deckle preferred, chopped**

3 cans (14.75 oz. size) **creamed corn**

1 can (16 oz.) **Bush's Baked Beans**

1 lb. **fresh lima beans or fresh string beans** (frozen is OK)

This stew is a two-day affair, usually reserved for larger parties because of the work it takes to do it right. If you ever see this recipe on anyone's menu... you will appreciate the work they went through to serve you this tasty stew! The day before, you will need to smoke your brisket overnight. The next morning, smoke off your chickens and twice smoke your sausage. I'm going to be up front with you... the quality of this stew is ultimately determined by the quality of your smoky beef brisket. You can short cut all of this by going to your local Famous Dave's BBQ Joint and buying all your pre-smoked meats! The slow-smoked meats are what pack this stew full of flavors... something you can't achieve by tossing raw meat into a kettle! The results are worth taking the time to use smoked meats.

Dice bacon and cook it off in a large skillet until crispy. Set bacon aside and drain, leaving 2 tablespoons of bacon grease.

In the empty bacon pan, sauté onions, celery, jalapeño, minced garlic, and bell pepper until the onions start to caramelize.

Move sautéed veggies to a large stock pot and add chicken stock, beef consommé, bacon, potatoes, crushed tomatoes, BBQ sauce, Worcestershire sauce, salt, pepper, and cayenne pepper and bring to a rolling simmer.

Add brisket and sausage and let simmer for 1/2 hour. Add creamed corn, baked beans, and lima beans or green beans, and bring to simmer about 15 minutes. Fold in chicken and let simmer for another 15 minutes.

This stew is best if made the day before.

# The Best Tailgating Chili Bowl!

**Not your average bowl of red!** This is an award-winning bowl of passionately created robust flavors that will warm yer innerds and leave you lickin' yer lips! This chili is perfect for any game day party or tailgating get-together. I have worked years fully devoted to perfecting this chili and it's guaranteed to have everyone wanting seconds! Served with your choice of diced onions, shredded cheddar cheese, diced avocados, or a dollop of sour cream. Top with **Cornbread Croutons** (pg. 197) to make this chili even more impressive!

## Delightfully serves a party of 8

3 lbs. 80/20 ground chuck

4 Tbsp. Superior Touch Better Than Bouillon Beef Base

1 cup sweet onion, diced

1 cup green bell pepper, diced

1 cup celery, diced

3 Tbsp. chili powder

2 Tbsp. +1 tsp. cumin

1 tsp. garlic powder

1 Tbsp. sweet basil (rubbed and broken down in your fist... do NOT use fresh)

1/2 tsp. kosher salt

1/2 tsp. fresh ground black pepper

1/2 tsp. crushed red pepper flakes

1/4 tsp. celery salt

32 oz. Spicy Hot V8 juice

1/4 cup Lea & Perrin's Worcestershire Sauce New Thick Style

8 oz. Hunt's Tomato Puree

14.5 oz. Hunt's Petite Diced Tomatoes

1 cup purified water (not tap or spring water)

1 can (16 oz.) Bush's Baked Beans Original Recipe

1 can (16 oz.) Bush's Black Beans (do not drain)

1 oz. Nestle's Unsweetened Chocolate

1 oz. Kahlua

In a large sauté pan, flatten out the ground chuck and add the beef base. Brown the meat, but don't be tempted to crush up the beef. Leave in big chunks as much as possible, but make sure it is thoroughly cooked. You want to get a fair amount of browning on the meat, as this adds flavor and texture. Once cooked, transfer the meat to a large stockpot and leave juices in the pan.

In the remaining juices, sauté onions, peppers, and celery. Once the onions start to turn translucent, transfer veggies to the stockpot.

Add all the dry seasonings to the stock pot. Then add V8 juice, Worcestershire sauce, tomato puree, diced tomatoes, and water. Heat until juices start to simmer.

Add beans carefully, try not to bust them. Return to a simmer; add chocolate and Kahlua. Simmer on low heat for 15 minutes.

This chili tastes best if held overnight, but either way it is awesome!

### This chili is exploding with flavor that will shoot sparks from your mouth!

# Creamy Potato & Corn Chowder

**I swear if everyone ate this soup all at once there would be world peace!** This is a great "feel good" soup that just wonderfully makes everything in the world seem to be OK. Pure nostalgia in a bowl, especially if you serve it with a slice of honey-buttered corn bread.

**Delightfully serves a party of 8**

**5 cups chicken stock**

**2 Knorr Chicken Bouillon Cubes**
(not granules)

**1 cup hickory-smoked bacon, chopped**

**1 cup hickory-smoked ham, chopped***

**1 cup onion, finely chopped**

**1/2 cup celery, finely chopped**

**2 tsp. fresh garlic, finely minced**

**3 Tbsp. butter**

**1/2 cup all-purpose flour**

**2 cups fresh grilled sweet corn**

**1 tsp. fresh ground black pepper**

**1 tsp. sea salt**

**1/4 tsp. celery seed**

**1/8 tsp. dill**

**1-1/2 tsp. dried parsley or
1 Tbsp. fresh parsley, finely chopped**

**3 lbs. diced baked potato**

**6 oz. half & half**

**6 oz. heavy whipping cream**

**12 oz. Carnation Evaporated Milk**

**1 cup Crystal Farms Sharp Cheddar**

**1 cup Cabot Vermont White Cheddar**

**grated sharp cheddar** (garnish)

**bacon pieces, chopped** (garnish)

**green onions or scallions, thinly sliced** (garnish)

*****Purchase a good quality single packaged ham steak**

Heat chicken stock in a large stockpot and add the chicken bouillon.

In a pan, fry bacon till crisp. Remove bacon and set aside. Then fry ham in the grease to add a nice brown caramel color to the ham. Remove ham and set aside. Reserve 3 tablespoons of bacon grease.

In a second stock pot, add reserved grease, onion, celery, and garlic and cook over medium heat until onions are translucent and celery is soft. Add butter and melt. Add flour and mix well. (You are making a vegetable roux.) Over low heat, cook the roux mixture for several minutes to make sure the flour is well cooked into the grease.

Slowly add chicken stock while mixing thoroughly. Bring mixture up to temp before you add more stock. Once mixed, add bacon, ham, sweet corn, pepper, salt, celery seed, dill, and parsley.

Add potatoes and whip aggressively very briefly…just enough to break up a few potatoes to add some thickness to the soup. (Be careful not to turn the soup into total mush!)

Add half & half, heavy whipping cream, and evaporated milk. Raise temperature and heat until hot enough to melt cheese. Stir constantly. Add cheeses and mix well. Bring to a low simmer and then serve immediately.

Serve garnished with grated sharp cheddar, bacon pieces, and thinly sliced green onions.

What makes this recipe tasty is the fresh seasonings and the quality of all the ingredients. The chicken broth should be made with a good full-flavored chicken base. Make sure the bacon is a good quality hickory-flavored bacon as this is a major flavor base in the soup… the same goes for the ham. It's the attention to detail with every single ingredient and correctness of dices and chops that make this soup so wonderful.

This soup is best if held overnight. It will tighten up and the seasonings will be full flavored the next day.

**Yields** 5 quarts or 10 – 16 oz. bowls of soup

## Famous Dave's Hot Tips!

Never boil cream roux-based soups—the soup will "break" and the fat will separate. Bring to a low simmer until soup reaches temperature.

# White Chicken Chili

**Someone really loves you when they make home-made soups, from scratch, using only the freshest ingredients.** This is a great, delicious soup that will make you fall in love all over again. It's old-fashioned comfort food with a kick!

---

### Delightfully serves a party of 10

64 oz. full-flavored homemade chicken stock*

2-1/2 tsp. cumin

1/4 tsp. fresh ground black pepper

1 cup carrot, finely grated

1 cup celery, finely chopped

1 cup sweet onion, finely chopped

6 Tbsp. butter

6 Tbsp. all-purpose flour

16 oz. pepper jack cheese, grated

3 cans (15.8 oz. size) **Bush's Great Northern Beans, drained**

2 cans (11 oz. size) **Green Giant White Shoepeg Corn or sweet corn niblets, drained**

3 lbs. chicken (I usually buy a rotisserie chicken from the grocery store)

8 oz. heavy cream

24 oz. half & half

16 oz. Pace medium salsa

*I like Progresso's chicken stock, if I don't have time to make my own.

In a stock pot, make chicken stock and mix in cumin and black pepper. Bring the stock to a good simmer; you do not want a rolling boil.

Remove chicken from bones and hand-tear into pieces. I like to throw the bones and the skin into the chicken stock, then hand-tear the meat into bite-size pieces. I don't like dicing the meat with a knife as it looks too commercial. Hand-torn chicken looks more rustic and homemade in the soup... to me it is the attention to detail that makes a great impression on the people you love.

In a sauté pan, add carrots, celery, onion and butter. Sauté until translucent. Mix flour into the sautéed veggies and make a roux. Remove bones and skin from stock. Slowly add 1/2 cup chicken stock into the roux while stirring vigorously with a gravy whisk. Let the roux return to a simmer before adding more stock, repeating until the mixture becomes like a thin gravy. Then empty the sauté pan into the stock pot with the rest of the chicken stock.

Bring stock pot to a slow simmer, add cheese and mix well. Add beans and corn, then return to a low simmer.

Add chicken, creams, and salsa; return to a simmer. (Add the chicken last because the constant stirring tends to shred the chicken.) Check saltiness and adjust.

**Yields** 10 – 16 oz. bowls of soup.

What do firemen put in their soup?

"Firecrackers."

# The Best Burger in America!

**This is the absolute best burger in America... guaranteed!** The perfect burger tastes beefy and has a nice crunch on the outside, but is tender and juicy on the inside. Out of all the sandwiches in the world... the All-American Classic Burger is everyone's favorite. From time to time everyone wonders what to eat and when they can't make up their mind... a burger always satisfies the soul.

---

### Delightfully serves a hungry party of 6!

3 lbs. 80/20 ground chuck

12 slices of bacon

lettuce, tomato, onion

6 slices aged cheddar cheese

6 bakery-fresh buns, buttered and toasted

50/50 kosher salt and fresh ground black pepper

This is probably the longest dissertation on how to make the best hamburger. I am doing this because burgers are the #1 most consumed sandwich in America and not everyone knows how to make the best burger! First, there is only one way to cook a burger... on a flat-top griddle. There is an on-going battle between charred-grilled burgers and flat-top grilled burgers about which one tastes better. All I can say is every restaurant anywhere in America that has ever been recognized for "The Best Burger in Town!" cooks their burgers on a flat-top grill. The burger marinates in it's own juices. A burger that is char-grilled over an open fire generally is not as moist. While a few people like rare burgers... I am advocating it's always best to grill your burgers to medium... just trust me. Every detail is important—from the time you get your meat from the butcher and your bun specifications, to how you cook and plate your burger. They say the devil is in the details... I say God is in the details and when you taste one of my heavenly burgers you'll know without a doubt you've been blessed!

## HOT BUTTERED BUNS

Use a fresh bakery bun from your favorite bakery; be creative—offering a variety of onion, brioche, sesame, or poppy seed buns to create pleasant surprises for family and friends. The biggest reason I am an advocate for fresh bakery buns is... in order to get a good golden buttery crustiness, YOU need to slice the bun fresh. Precut buns typically dry out and the interior of the buns start "cupping," which causes the buns to only toast on the edges, leaving the interior soggy!

## Famous Dave's Hot Tips!

How to Avoid the SOGGY BUN!
Butter your buns with soft butter and toast them face down on a hot griddle. Make sure to get your buns good and toasted to a dark crusty golden brown. A perfectly toasted buttered bun will hold up to the juiciest burger; the crunchy buttery texture adds to your guest's "Total Mouth Experience" when they bite into your burger.

*Whenever I have friends over for a party and serve burgers, my friends always say, "Dave, you have nice buns!"*

## THE BURGER MEAT

Order fresh ground meat directly from your butcher—especially when planning a family get-together or party. 80/20 ground chuck is the best meat selection to ensure the right ratio of meat to fat, which is needed for flavor in the burger... much like a well-marbled steak. Get 3lb trays and tell your butcher to lay the meat "loosely" in the meat tray. You don't want packed meat! Study the meat photo... see how loosely packed this hamburger is lying in the tray? This is what you want from the butcher. I can't tell you how important this is and I'll emphasize it more when we get to making the patty. When you grill your meat, you want the flavors to travel throughout the inside of the burger; if your burger is packed too tightly, the juices will run out rather than getting trapped within the patty.

## MAKING THE PATTY: Don't play with your meat!!!

When making a patty... Don't play with your meat!
You want to handle it the least amount you can. Don't make the meat into a perfect round ball. Just grab a good handful (6-8oz) and with just a few hand motions lightly roll it into a roughly shaped ball. With ONE single push of the palm of your hand, flatten the ball. It's important that you leave your ball roughly shaped because the craggy rough edges will brown and caramelize with flavor. These rough, misshapen edges remind me of the rough craggy fjords of Norway! The flavorful crispy edges of the meat create the first impression when your guests take their first bite. By not packing the meat, the juices are free to float in the burger and marinate your meat. Anywhere from 6 to 10 ounces of meat per burger is the typical size for a patty; I recommend you select your burger size based on the size of your bun.

## SEASONING THE BURGER

Many people think they have to add lots of spices or flavorings to make the perfect burger. Actually, the two seasonings for grilling the best-tasting burger are simply kosher salt and freshly ground black pepper. Fresh ground pepper is so important; don't be lazy and use the stuff that's been sitting on the shelf for months. AND DON'T GET CRAZY WITH SEASONINGS TO TRY AND PROVE YOU'RE SOME KIND OF FOODIE. It should always be your goal... "to get a great-tasting burger that tastes like a burger." Don't confuse your guests about what's in the meat!

*Option: If you don't have a problem with MSG (or Accent), by all means lightly sprinkle your meat with Accent, which is a great meat and seasoning flavor enhancer.*

## COOKING YOUR BURGER

I like to use a large cast iron griddle that fits over two gas burners. A big heavy pan is fine, too. You want to have a hot pan or griddle. I always have some beef fat handy and I melt beef fat right on the griddle. Quickly sear your burger, getting a nice, caramelized brown, seared burger by sealing in all the flavored juices.

Place your patty on the griddle with the seasoning side facing up. Do NOT put the seasoning side down first! As your burger cooks, the seasonings on the top side will marinate the meat.

### DON'T EVER SMASH YOUR BURGER WITH A SPATULA!

When you do this you smash out all the flavorful juices. In my restaurants, I will fire someone if I ever catch them smashing a burger with a spatula… that's how serious I am about smashing! Don't flip the burger until the juices start to pool on top of the burger. This means your meat has nicely caramelized on the bottom. It is so important not to smash your burger when you're forming it, because burgers that have been smashed too much don't pool juices on the top while cooking like a lightly formed burger pools juices.

Once you flip your burger, add cheese and cook it just until you see the bottom edges start to turn lightbrown. If you want… you can sprinkle water on the griddle and cover. The steam will help quickly melt your cheese. Your burger is done!

*Famous Dave's Favorite Burger… BBQ Sauce, Hickory-Smoked Bacon, Sharp Cheddar Cheese, and Hell Fire Pickles*

## SAUCE TOPPINGS

Here's where to have some fun. Don't just provide plain ketchup and mustard. Puree a jar of pickled jalapeño peppers and add ketchup for a tangy Jalapeño Ketchup with a kick. Provide an assortment of mustards like Dijon mustard, stone-ground mustard, and honey mustard. AND Famous Dave's BBQ Sauce is always an excellent choice to have on the table!

## ASSORTED TOPPINGS

If you really want to see people's eyes light up, have an assortment of cheeses, coleslaw, grilled pineapple, hickory-smoked bacon, green olives, and a variety of pickles alongside your traditional toppings of lettuce, tomatoes, and onions.

# Smoked Turkey Panini
## Mmm... Mmm... Mmm...

### slathered with BLUEBERRY Chipotle Mayo

**Go ahead and lick the page! Yes, this sandwich is that tasty!!!** Beautiful smoked turkey floating on Blueberry Chipotle Mayo topped with fresh spinach, juicy tomatoes and dairy, delicious gruyere cheese…creates the most unbelievably tasty sandwich. What makes this sandwich so tasty and fun to eat is the crispiness of the buttery-toasted sourdough bread. The Panini grill makes a delicious, wonderful, crunchy difference. And the Blueberry Chipotle Mayo ROCKS! Once you get a taste of this blueberry flavored mayo… you're going to be plastering this stuff over everything you eat!

**Delightfully serves a party of 6**

**3 lb. turkey breast** (you'll have leftovers)

**1/2 recipe of All-Purpose Charcoal Grill Chicken Seasoning** (pg. 145)

**1 loaf sourdough bread, sliced**

**Blueberry Chipotle Mayo**

**8 oz. fresh spinach leaves**

**1 lb. Gruyere cheese**

**4 tomatoes**

**1 stick unsalted melted butter or 1/2 cup olive oil**

Prepare grill with charcoal and several chunks of hickory wood covered in aluminum. Rub turkey breast with chicken seasoning; best if marinated overnight. Smoke chicken at 300 to 325 degrees for 2 hours or until meat reaches an internal temperature of 170. Let cool and slice thin. Turn on Panini grill.

Spread **Blueberry Chipotle Mayo** over slices of sourdough bread. Layer with smoked turkey, spinach leaves, tomato slices, and slices of Gruyere cheese. Slather butter on bread and place buttered side down on hot Panini grill and then quickly slather the top slice of bread with butter, and close Panini grill.

**NOTE:** the number of sandwiches you get out of this recipe depends on the size of your sourdough bread.

# Blueberry Chipotle Mayo

**1 pint blueberries**

**1 cup mayo**

**1 tsp. Aleppo chili pepper**

**1/2 tsp. chipotle pepper in adobo sauce**

**1/4 tsp. salt**

Puree blueberries and mix into mayo. Add Aleppo chili pepper, chipotle pepper, and salt and mix well. Refrigerate mayo.

Best if made the day before.

### Famous Dave's 'Que & A

**'Que:** if a recipe calls for only a teaspoon of chipotle peppers, what kind should I buy?

**Answer:** Chipotle peppers are really just dried, smoked Jalapeño peppers. The two most common forms are a ground chipotle powder or a wet chipotle pepper. I prefer the wet chipotle pepper in adobo sauce, as the flavor is so much more intense... but the smallest size can available is 7 ounces. The secret to using chipotle pepper in adobo sauce is finding your own favorite brand. There are several Hispanic brands and some are hot and some are mild. The adobo sauce varies greatly, as well. Adobo sauces can be tangy, spicy, or mildly sweet. Find the one that best suits your taste buds to create your recipes. Since most recipes don't require a lot of chipotle seasoning, I usually buy the small size can, puree everything, place it in an empty jelly jar, and keep it in my refrigerator until I need it.

# The Grand Slam-mich
## Twice Smoked Sausage & Spicy Coleslaw

**You'll score big with this tailgate winner!** The grandstands will be cheering as hungry fans tackle this robust, flavor-punched sandwich. It's a sure bet for any tailgate party. What makes this "Grand Slam-mich" everyone's favorite is making sure the bun is buttery toasted, twice smoking the sausage, a spicy yellow coleslaw, and Famous Dave's Spicy Pickles. There's no fumbling here… sports fans will go hog wild over this major league taste sensation!

**Delightfully serves a party of 8**

## SPICY YELLOW COLESLAW

1 head cabbage, shredded

1 cup mayonnaise

1/4 cup yellow mustard

1/4 cup sugar

1 Tbsp. Sriracha hot chili sauce

1/2 tsp. salt

1 tsp. white pepper

## GRAND SLAM-MICH

8 hot italian sausages ***

1 jar of Famous Dave's Spicy Pickle Chips

8 bakery hamburger buns

butter

*** I highly recommend you find the best fresh, tasty, hot Italian sausages at your local grocer.

---

Mix all ingredients for **Spicy Yellow Coleslaw** and refrigerate until use.

"There are two things you are going to be doing with your grill and sausages…first, you are going to get a nice smoke on your sausages. Second, you are going to split the sausages and place them on a hot grill to get a good char."

Start a small charcoal fire in your grill and when the coals are hot add several aluminum-covered hickory wood chunks… work to get a good smoke going. Your smoker should be about 225 degrees. Smoke your sausages until they have a golden brown smokiness and start to bubble a clear juice; this takes about a half hour depending on the temperature of your grill.

Take the sausages off and add another chimney full of hot charcoal to your grill and get it real hot. Slice the smoked sausages lengthwise and put them back on the hot grill to get a decent char on the sausages, adding another layer of flavor.

While you smoke your sausages, take the bakery buns and get them good and buttered. Once your sausages are done, put your buns on the grill grates until they are a toasty golden brown. Don't under-toast your buns! Part of the success of this tasty sandwich is getting a good buttery crusted bun that will hold up under the sogginess of the coleslaw. The grill will be very hot, so watch your buns closely so they don't burn.

On a butter-toasted bun, place the split sausage flat on the bun and pile on the coleslaw. Top this with Famous Dave's Spicy Pickle Chips. You're going to love this "slam-mich!"

# Grilled Coney Island Dogs

**Truly "The Ultimate Hot Dog"... authentic grilled Coney Island Hot Dogs!** I'm not talking about chili dogs (there is a difference!). The old-fashioned, amusement park flavor will make your taste buds think you're on New York's famous Coney Island boardwalk back in the 1940s! Natural casing hot dogs on buttery toasted, bakery buns make this Coney Island Hot Dog a winner. A slathering of yellow mustard is a must... don't even think of using some fancy-schmancy mustard here! Then the dog is topped with real Coney Island meat sauce, and a generous heaping of finely minced onions—all crowned with a mound of finely-grated sharp cheddar cheese. This beauty of a sandwich is great for parties and your guests will marvel... "We've never tasted a hot dog so incredibly mouthwateringly delicious."

**Delightfully serves a party of 12**

2 packages natural casing hot dogs

12 bakery fresh hot dog buns (NOT pre-sliced hot dog buns)

2 large white or yellow onions, minced

1 bottle yellow mustard

1 lb. sharp cheddar cheese, finely grated

# CONEY ISLAND MEAT SAUCE

2 lbs. 85/15 ground chuck

4 cups pure filtered water

2 Tbsp. Superior Touch "Better Than Beef Bouillon" Beef Base

1 small pack of Swanson's Flavor Boost Beef Flavor

2 Tbsp. Famous Dave's Rich & Sassy BBQ Sauce

2 Tbsp. white vinegar

1 Tbsp. Hunt's Tomato Paste

1 Tbsp. dry minced onion

1/2 tsp. dry minced garlic

2 tsp. dry sweet basil, crushed

1 tsp. chili powder

1 tsp. fresh fine ground black pepper

1/4 tsp. cayenne pepper

1/2 tsp. celery seed

*This meat sauce elevates the common hot dog to something close to a National treasure!*

Prepare the **Coney Island Meat Sauce**. Do not buy prepackaged ground chuck or hamburger if at all possible. Ask your butcher to make you fresh 85/15 fine ground burger mix. Place the burger meat in a large sauce pan. Add four cups water to the meat and with your hands… (yes, you need to use your "clean" hands for this—or wear disposable kitchen gloves). Using your hands, break up the meat in the water until it is a meaty slush. Over high heat, bring to a slow boil. Using a skimmer, remove the grayish foam on top of the water as the meat cooks. Once the foam subsides, add the rest of the meat sauce ingredients. Once the mixture returns to a slight rolling boil, reduce heat to low and continue simmering. Simmer for 1 hour while stirring frequently; do not cover.

Slice the buns down the top. Butter the sides and grill to a rich dark golden brown. The buns are best with a heavier toast because it makes the bun firmer to hold.

Grill hot dogs until they are darkened and ready to split. Place grilled hot dogs on toasted buns, slather with yellow mustard, generously top with meat sauce, and finely minced onion, and lastly… mound finely grated cheddar cheese on top. Enjoy!

"PRETTY in PINK"

# SMOKIN' BUFFALO CHICKEN SANDWICH

## This sandwich rocks... It's a barbecue party on a bun!

**The average person has 10,000 taste buds and this sandwich will WOW everyone of them!** If you're wondering what to serve at your next tailgating party, this is a great-tasting sandwich that will spike up the action! Your fans will love the smoky rotisserie chicken, Wasabi Buffalo Mayo, hickory-smoked bacon, Buffalo Drizzling Sauce, Pepper Jack Cheese Sauce, and my Famous Dave's Spicy Pickles piled on a toasted hoagie bun. This sandwich is flavor spanked with deliciousness!

---

### Delightfully serves a party of 4

1 lb. hickory smoked bacon

1 rotisserie smoked chicken

8 oz. sharp cheddar cheese, shredded

1 jar Famous Dave's Spicy Pickles

4 hoagie buns, buttered and toasted

kosher salt (to taste)

fresh ground pepper (to taste)

Wasabi Buffalo Mayo

Buffalo Drizzling Sauce

Pepper Jack Cheese Sauce

Cook off bacon and set aside. Smoke a rotisserie chicken for best results or if you don't have time buy a rotisserie chicken from your local supermarket. Pull chicken apart and leave it in large pieces as best as possible.

Prepare the **Wasabi Buffalo Mayo**, **Buffalo Drizzling Sauce**, and **Pepper Jack Cheese Sauce**.

Slice hoagie buns in half, butter and toast. Slather each side of the hoagie bun with a generous dollop of **Wasabi Buffalo Mayo**. Layer on the pulled chicken and season with salt and pepper to taste. Drizzle chicken with drizzling sauce. Next layer with bacon. Generously sauce with melted cheese sauce. Top it all off with spicy pickles..

## WASABI BUFFALO MAYO

1/2 cup mayonnaise

4 oz. cream cheese, softened

4 oz. sour cream

1 Tbsp. Louisiana Hot Sauce

1 Tbsp. Texas Pete's Hot Sauce or Frank's Red Hot Sauce

2 Tbsp. Asian sweet chili sauce

1 Tbsp. blue agave honey

2 tsp. Wasabi horseradish paste

Mix all ingredients together and place in refrigerator for 2 hours to set.

## BUFFALO DRIZZLING SAUCE

2 Tbsp. Louisiana Hot Sauce

2 Tbsp. Texas Pete's Hot Sauce or Frank's Hot Sauce

In a small bowl, mix ingredients together to create sauce and place in a squeeze bottle.

---

## PEPPER JACK CHEESE SAUCE

2 cups pepper jack cheese, shredded

2 cups sharp cheddar cheese, shredded

1/2 cup half & half

In a double broiler, place pepper jack cheese, cheddar cheese, and half & half; heat on medium heat. Cook until melted and well blended; stir occasionally.

This sandwich is so tasty, your tongue will jump out of your mouth and lick your eyebrows!

# Grilled Margarita Chipotle Chicken Sandwich
## with Pineapple Mango Salsa

**Yes, it is 5 o'clock somewhere... and after tasting this Margarita Chipotle Chicken Sandwich you'll never search for your lost salt shaker again!** Margarita Chipotle marinated chicken breasts topped with **Pineapple Mango Salsa** and served on a grilled toasty bun will have you thinking you're out in Kokomo wearing your best flowered shirt and sandals. This sandwich is fruity, spicy, and refreshingly light.

**Delightfully serves a party of 6**

**6 chicken breasts**

**Famous Dave's Fish Seasoning** (pg. 173)

**6 small loaves French bread**

**garlic butter**

**lettuce** (I used romaine for this sandwich but any lettuce will do)

**olive oil**

# MARGARITA CHIPOTLE MARINADE

**1 cup margarita mix** (I like Margaritaville's Margarita Mix)

**1/2 cup fresh lime juice**

**1/2 cup fresh orange juice**

**2 Tbsp. packed fresh cilantro, finely minced**

**1 Tbsp. garlic cloves, minced & smashed**

**2 tsp. sea salt**

**2 tsp. granulated garlic**

**1 Tbsp. granulated onion**

**1/4 tsp. coarse ground black pepper**

**1 tsp. chipotle pepper in adobo sauce, pureed**

**Yields 2-1/3 cups of marinade**

# PINEAPPLE MANGO SALSA

**2 mangos, diced**

**1-1/2 cups pineapple, chopped**

**2 avocados, diced**

**1 red bell pepper, diced**

**1/2 cup red onion, diced**

**1/2 tsp. chipotle pepper in adobo sauce, pureed**

**1 Tbsp. fresh cilantro, finely minced**

**2 Tbsp. fresh lime juice**

**2 tsp. Ball Fruit-Fresh Produce Protector**

Ideally, two days prior to serving, prepare the **Margarita Chipotle Marinade** to allow the flavors to fully bloom. Mix all marinade ingredients and seal in an airtight container. Refrigerate.

One day prior, on a clean cutting board, place chicken breasts and, using a meat hammer, softly pound them. You do NOT want to flatten them, only even them out. In addition, the pounding will break the muscle fibers so the meat absorbs the marinade better. In a large plastic bag, place pounded chicken breasts and marinade. Refrigerate overnight. Turn chicken over halfway through your marinade time.

Start your grill with chunks of hickory wood. Remove the chicken from the marinade. Shake off excess marinade; discard marinade. Place chicken on a plate and season with **Famous Dave's Fish Seasoning** (pg. 173). Pour some olive oil on plate and toss chicken in the olive oil to coat.

Prepare **Pineapple Mango Salsa** right before you grill the chicken to keep it as fresh as possible. Or you can prepare everything except the avocados and add them at the last minute so they don't brown on you.

Place the chicken on a smoky grill and cover. Grill on each side for about 8 minutes. Chicken is done when the juices are clear. Slice chicken breasts on a bias.

Start assembling sandwiches by slicing French loaves and slathering them with garlic butter. I usually toast the bread on my grill before grilling my chicken; you have to be very careful as it doesn't take long before you end up with charred pieces of toast. If you don't trust yourself… just toast them under your oven's broiler. Place lettuce on the baguettes and layer the chicken on top. Top with a generous helping of **Pineapple Mango Salsa**.

Prepare all fruits and veggies except for the avocados and lime juice. Once everything is prepared… mix Ball Fruit-Fresh Produce Protector with the lime juice.

Dice avocados. Splash and gently toss with the Fruit Fresh lime juice. Gently mix avocados into the rest of the fruits and veggies.

If this salsa is not going to be served right away, take a piece of plastic wrap and place it directly on the salsa. Gently push the plastic wrap down into the salsa so there are no air pockets, this will prevent your salsa from turning brown. Refrigerate until needed.

# El BBQ Fiesta!

# BBQ Pork Tacos

**Here's a fun party recipe… BBQ Tacos!** My BBQ Pork Tacos feature smoky pulled BBQ pork, baked beans, BBQ Pico de Gallo, and a beautiful lip smackin' red cabbage spicy coleslaw… topped with sprinkles of goat cheese. These hand-held tacos are colorful, tasty, and fun to eat… Great Party Food!

## Delightfully serves a party of 5

**15 oz. Bush's Original Baked Beans**

**1/4 c. Famous Dave's Texas Pit BBQ Sauce**

**10 corn or flour tortillas**

**2 lb. BBQ smoked pork, hand shredded**

**1 recipe of BBQ Pico de Gallo** (pg. 55)

**1 recipe of Sriracha Red Cabbage Coleslaw** (pg. 196)

**8 oz goat cheese crumbles**

In a small bowl, mix the baked beans with the BBQ sauce. In this picture, I pureed the baked beans with the BBQ sauce and used it like a bean paste on the tortilla… you may puree the beans or just use them whole… whatever you prefer.

Grill your tortillas over a medium hot grill. Be careful—it only takes but a couple of seconds to warm up these fragile tortillas.

Layer about 3 ounces of hand-shredded pulled pork. I always like to smoke my own BBQ meats for flavor intensity and freshness. If you don't have time, I highly recommend you stop off at your closest Famous Dave's and pick up a couple of pounds of our famous Georgia Chopped Pork!

Next, spoon the **BBQ Pico de Gallo** over the pork and top this with my **Sriracha Red Cabbage Coleslaw**. Sprinkle goat cheese on top… and you are in for a real tasty treat!

You can also drizzle some Famous Dave's BBQ Sauce on top or add a dollop of sour cream or my fabulous **Festive Party Guacamole** (pg. 56).

**Yields:** 10 good-sized tacos.

# REDNECKIN' HILLBILLY TACOS

**There's something magical when you top Johnny Cakes with BBQ Smoky Chicken, Spicy Coleslaw, and Pickled Red Onions!** This is real down-home Southern comfort food done righteous. The gritty white cornmeal Johnny Cakes or "hoecakes" were originally a Southern staple made out in the field on a hoe held over an open fire. Fire up yer griddle and stack 'em up... serve these Redneckin' Hillbilly Tacos with fresh-squeezed lemonade or sweet tea for the perfect appetizer or light lunch!

**Delightfully serves a party of 6**

**Spicy Yellow Coleslaw** (pg. 115)

**Pickled Red Onions**

**1 smoked rotisserie chicken, hand pulled** (pg. 145)

**Johnny Cakes**

**1/2 cup Famous Dave's BBQ Sauce**

At least 8 hours prior, prepare **Spicy Yellow Coleslaw** and **Pickled Red Onions**. Smoke and hand pull a rotisserie chicken. In a bowl, toss chicken with 1/2 cup Famous Dave's BBQ Sauce.

Prepare **Johnny Cakes**. Place a Johnny Cake on a plate, layer on rotisserie chicken, then Spicy Yellow Coleslaw, and top with Pickled Red Onions. Drizzle with Famous Dave's BBQ Sauce.

## JOHNNY CAKES OR HOECAKES

**1-1/2 cups water**

**1 tsp. salt**

**1 Tbsp. sugar**

**2 Tbsp. bacon drippings or melted butter**

**2 eggs, beaten**

**1-2/3 cup self-rising white cornmeal flour***

**1/3 cup white cornmeal**

**Crisco oil for frying**

***I recommend using White Lily self-rising white cornmeal flour.**

Heat Crisco oil in a non-stick griddle to medium heat.

Mix all ingredients and ladle batter onto griddle. Fry until well browned on edges before turning.

Makes 8 appetizer-sized hoecakes.

## PICKLED RED ONIONS

**1 large red onion**

**1/4 cup brined jalapeño peppers, drained**

**1-1/2 cups apple cider vinegar**

**1/2 cup apple juice concentrate**

**1/4 cup light brown sugar**

**1/4 tsp. canning salt**

Peel onion, cut in half and core. Cut into 1/8-inch thin slices. Slice jalapeños. Place onion and jalapeño slices in a covered plastic container.

In a 5-quart stock pot, place vinegar, apple juice concentrate, brown sugar, and salt. Heat pickling mixture over medium heat, stirring constantly until sugar has dissolved. This should take about 7 minutes. Remove from heat and let rest for one hour.

Pour pickling mixture over onions and jalapeños; mix together. Cover and place in refrigerator for at least 8 hours before serving.

# Cranberry Smoked Chicken Lettuce Wraps

**Simple, Crispy, Cool, and Refreshing!** These Cranberry Smoked Chicken Lettuce Wraps are the perfect summer party food…they are fun to make and fun to eat. Tasty rotisserie smoked chicken, green grapes, dried cranberries, tomatoes, sweet onions, and celery topped off with toasted slivers of crunchy almonds make this recipe perfect for quick get-togethers. The vanilla-flavored yogurt combines with the mayo for a surprisingly delicious dressing.

## Delightfully serves a party of 8

1/2 cup mayonnaise

1/2 cup vanilla yogurt (not Greek)

1/4 tsp. paprika

1/2 tsp. seasoned salt

1/4 tsp. fresh ground black pepper

1/2 cup seedless green grapes, halved

1/2 cup dried cranberries

1/2 cup celery, sliced

1/2 cup sweet onions, minced

1/2 cup toasted almond slivers

1 smoked rotisserie chicken, hand shredded (pg. 145)

2 small tomatoes, diced

2 heads butter leaf lettuce

In a medium bowl, mix together mayonnaise, yogurt, paprika, seasoned salt, and black pepper. Mix in grapes, dried cranberries, celery, onion, and almonds.

Add chicken and tomatoes last and gently mix well. I recommend that you hand shred the chicken instead of making it look "blocky" by cutting the chicken with a knife. Be careful not to over-shred the chicken. The salad looks better if the chicken doesn't look stringy. Place lettuce cups (see **Hot Tip**, below) on a platter and scoop chicken salad into the lettuce.

This recipe is incredibly tasty when you smoke your own rotisserie chicken. Your guests will go nuts over the mouthwatering flavor. However, IF YOU MUST… this recipe is very simply done by buying a rotisserie chicken.

## Famous Dave's Hot Tips!

You'll need 2 heads of lettuce to find suitably sized lettuce leaves for a wrap. Use the leftover lettuce for a party salad. Lettuce is not always cooperative… so I get my lettuce to shape up and behave! I pick out the best leaves, then I get a tomato or other round fruit like apples or oranges. Next, I lay a piece of plastic wrap down, then lay a wet paper towel on top and start layering my lettuce on the wet towel. When I have enough lettuce, I place a tomato in the middle and then fold the wet towel around it. Then pull the plastic wrap around everything to hold it in place. This can be done a day before your party, so your lettuce will be in the perfect "cup shape" for lettuce wraps!

# ROMAINE TURKEY TACOS

**Here's a quick, light, and savory treat everyone will love.** These hand-held Romaine Turkey Tacos are flavorful and delicious, but the best part is… they're healthy! Smoked turkey, fresh grilled corn, black beans, and diced Roma tomatoes served on a crisp Romaine lettuce leaf, topped with savory Añejo Cotija Mexican cheese crumbles, and drizzled with my BBQ Mayo Sauce. The turkey can be smoked the day before your party, making these tacos quick and easy. Turkey tacos made with Romaine lettuce make a great appetizer or are filling enough for lunch or a light dinner.

## Delightfully serves a party of 10

3 lbs. **smoked turkey breast**

3 heads of **Romaine lettuce**

1 can (15 oz.) **black beans**

3 - ears of fresh **corn** grilled or
1 can (15 oz.) **sweet corn niblets**

3 **Roma tomatoes**, diced

1 package of **Añejo Cotija cheese crumbles**

Pick through the Romaine lettuce to find the best leaves for your tacos.

Refer to the **Smoked Turkey Panini** recipe (pg. 113) for directions
on smoking the turkey breast. Hand shred the turkey into bite-size pieces. Prepare **BBQ Mayo Sauce**.

While smoking the turkey, place your fresh corn on the grill for 10 to 15 minutes until roasted. Then cut corn kernels off. If corn is not in season, you can use canned corn niblets. In a bowl, mix black beans, corn, and diced tomatoes together.

To build your tacos, place turkey on Romaine lettuce leaves and spoon corn and bean mixture over turkey. Sprinkle Cotija cheese crumbles over the tacos and drizzle BBQ Mayo Sauce on top.

## BBQ MAYO SAUCE

1/4 cup **sour cream**

1/4 cup **mayonnaise**

2 Tbsp. **Famous Dave's Rich & Sassy BBQ Sauce**

1 tsp **Louisiana Hot Sauce**

Mix sour cream, mayo, BBQ sauce, and hot sauce together. Place in a squirt bottle for drizzling.

# JIMMIE'S OLD SOUTHERN PULLED PORK SANDWICH

**America's Favorite BBQ Sandwich!** Slow smoked pulled pork, topped with a spicy Sriracha Red Cabbage Coleslaw, slathered with my award-winning BBQ sauce, and served on a buttery toasted bun. This is everyone's all-time favorite sandwich served with a pile of my Spicy Hell Fire Pickles and scrumptious corn fritters. This sandwich is named after my dad, "Jimmie Anderson," who loved his barbecue!

---

### Delightfully serves a party of 8

**2 lbs. The World's Best Smoked Pork Butt pulled** (pg. 132)

**Sriracha Red Cabbage Coleslaw** (pg. 196)

**Dave's Apricot Mustard BBQ Sauce**

**8 toasted buttered buns**

Prepare The World Best Smoked Pork Butt; this smoking process takes 10-12 hours. Prepare **Sriracha Red Cabbage Coleslaw** and **Dave's Apricot Mustard BBQ Sauce.**

Butter your buns and toast on a griddle or your grill. Once toasted, pile shards of the pork butt onto the buns. Drizzle a generous helping of the **Apricot Mustard BBQ Sauce** on the pork. Top with a good dollop of **Sriracha Red Cabbage Coleslaw**. Serve with my **Spicy Hell Fire Pickles** (pg. 194) and **Miss Mamie's Old Southern Corn Fritters** (pg. 187).

## DAVE'S APRICOT MUSTARD BBQ SAUCE

**1/2 cup Famous Dave's Rich and Sassy BBQ Sauce**

**1/2 cup Famous Dave's Georgia Mustard Sauce**

**1 cup Smucker's Apricot Preserves**

Mix everything together. Heat in an open pot in the smoker until simmering--do not boil. Remove and set aside.

# —Directions for Smoking the World's Best Smoked Pork Butt!

**Yeilds approximately 6 - 7 lbs.**

10 lb. pork butt

yellow mustard

brown sugar

1/4 cup turbinado or raw sugar

Jimmie's Old Southern Pork Butt Rub

Dave's Own Butt Juice Marinade

Dave's Spritzer Spray

**Use this great recipe for...**

Jimmie's Old Southern Pulled Pork Sandwiches (pg. 130)
BBQ Pork Tacos (pg. 123)
BBQ Nachos Grande (pg. 41)
BBQ Party in a Glass - 9-Layer BBQ Party Dip (pg. 73)

First, make the three recipes below... then follow the directions on the following pages for the World's Best Smoked Pork Butt EVER!

## JIMMIE'S OLD SOUTHERN PORK BUTT RUB

1/2 cup dark brown sugar

1/2 cup maple sugar

1/4 cup hickory-smoked salt, light colored version

1 Tbsp. fresh ground black pepper

1 Tbsp. celery salt

1 Tbsp. onion salt

1 tsp. cayenne pepper

1 tsp. chipotle pepper powder

1 Tbsp. Accent (optional)

To make this Pork Butt Rub you need to find a light-colored hickory-smoked salt. Do not use the dark versions. If you can't find the lighter version, go online and order it. Normally when making seasoning mixtures I never buy garlic salt or celery salt because I want the seasoning to be highlighted, but for Pork Butt Rubs I have found the flavored salts work better.

Mix all ingredients together and keep in an airtight plastic container or jar.

## DAVE'S OWN BUTT JUICE MARINADE

**Honestly I don't know what else to call it... it is what it says!**

8 cups Mott's Apple Juice or top quality fresh apple juice

2 cups apple juice concentrate

1/2 cup light brown sugar

3 Tbsp. Famous Dave's Steak Seasoning (pg. 143)

2 Tbsp. canning salt

2 Tbsp. Wright's Liquid Smoke (optional)

1/2 cup Frank's Hot Sauce

1 or 2 Tbsp. Accent, to taste (optional)

Mix ingredients together and place in your injector.

## DAVE'S SPRITZER SPRAY

1 cup apple juice

1/4 cup apple juice concentrate

1/4 cup apple cider vinegar

Combine ingredients and put in a bottle for spritzing.

**1** First, Pork Butts are really Pork Shoulders from the front of the pig and the name "Butt" has nothing to do with the anatomy of a hog. Back in the old days in New England, certain cuts of meat that were from the front of the hog were highly valued and hence the phrase "living high on the hog."

These cuts of meat were stored in wooden casks called "Butts." The folks in Boston started calling them Boston Butts... and today the name has stuck—although they're more commonly known as Pork Butts. Don't buy "boneless" pork butts. The bone provides a lot of flavor and when the butt is fully smoked this bone will fall right out.

**2** You will be injecting a marinade into your butt and this can get messy. Protect your kitchen by placing your butt fat side up in a tall plastic kitchen garbage bag and place this in a large tub. Roll the garbage bag down around the tub to give yourself good access to the butt.

Fill your injector with **Dave's Own Butt Juice Marinade** and reserve the rest of the marinade. Start injecting the marinade into the meat about every one inch.

**3** Score the fat like you would a fresh ham. Rub with a slathering of yellow mustard. The mustard acts like a paste to hold all the other seasonings.

**4** Cover the mustard with generous coating of dark brown sugar and rub around. Next, sprinkle **Jimmie's Old Southern Pork Butt Rub** over the brown sugar.

**5** Repeat the above seasoning procedure by flipping the butt over and covering the meat side with mustard and brown sugar. Next, coat the meat side of butt with Jimmie's Old Southern Pork Butt Rub. Then lightly but generously sprinkle raw sugar over this... your butt is now well seasoned and ready for the smoker.

**6** Next, prep your grill by placing an aluminum pan down and one pan facing up to collect juices. Place 1'' of water in the top pan.

This Is Important: You want to do this to collect the flavorful juices dripping from your butt.

**7** Place the butt fat side down in smoker at about 225 degrees. You want the fat side down, first because the fat keeps your marinade from oozing out. Place Hickory and Apple wood in a 50/50 combination, or try a combination of Hickory and Cherry wood. I also highly recommend using a remote thermometer as it allows you to work in your kitchen while watching the temperature of your butt.

**8** After the first hour, start spritzing meat with **Dave's Spritzer Spray**. Spritzing helps create the highly prized "sugar cookie" bark. About halfway through your smoke, or after 6 hours… give the entire butt another sprinkling of raw sugar to help keep building "bark" and turn the meat over so the fat side is up. Generously sprinkle raw sugar over the fat side. "Bark" is the caramelization that occurs on top of the meat as it smokes when the sugars blend with the meat juices and create that tasty sugar cookie crusty bark.

**9** A properly smoked butt will take between 10 and 12 hours—depending on your smoker. I would start checking your pork butt around 8 hours. Once the butt's inner temperature reaches 200 degrees, remove the butt and the drip pan. Place the pork butt meat side down into the butt juices and place this pan into an empty insulated cooler. Make a tent out of aluminum foil to cover the pork butt. Close the lid on the cooler to retain heat. After an hour, the butt should have sucked in some of the juices.

## Famous Dave's Hot Tips!

If after 6 hours you don't have the time to continue smoking… place your butt in a crock pot with BBQ sauce and cook until tender.

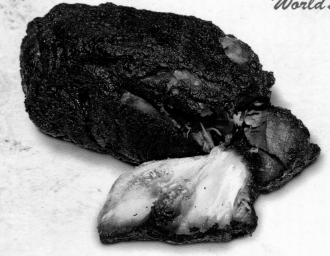

**10** After 12 hours, remove the pork butt from the drip pan and place on a cutting board. You can't help but notice in this picture how dark the pork butt has become. This dark covering over your butt is called "Bark." This bark is to die for…it is smoky, crusty and flavorful. If you were successful, your bark should taste like a smoky crusted sugar cookie! This pork butt may be be crusty on the outside but inside the meat is moist, juicy, and "Tender as a Mother's Love!"

**11** Pull the bone out... actually, it should almost fall out because the meat is so tender. Next, squash the butt tenderly with the flat of your hand. You want to keep the muscles intact as much as possible. Remove large fat chunks, but leave some "loose" tender fat to keep the meat nice and juicy. With rubber-gloved hands, pull meat apart and then chop the meat to the best eating size. Distribute the tasty "bark" throughout meat. DON'T OVER PULL YOUR PORK! Over pulling your pork will make it stringy. Many people make this mistake!

**12** Take saved juices in the bottom of the aluminum foil pan and mix this 50/50 with the reserved butt juice marinade that has NOT been used for injection or did NOT touch raw meat. Sprinkle this over the chopped pork for added flavor.

**13** Now here's the secret step that makes everything come together to create the best tasting pulled pork. Take some of the **Jimmie's Old Southern Pork Butt Rub** and place it in a coffee grinder and grind into a finer grind but don't over do it so it turns into powder. You are creating a "magic dust" for pork. Using a "fine" screened powder sugar shaker…fill shaker with ground rub and <u>lightly</u> sprinkle this over the chopped pork. This works better for flavor than sprinkling the original coarser rub, which would overwhelm the smokiness you worked so hard to achieve.

## Famous Dave's Hot Tips!

A 10-pound raw pork butt will typically yield 6-7 pounds of smoked meat. This mouthwatering smoked pork butt can be served by itself or used in any recipe that calls for a smoked and pulled meat.

The Original Famous Dave's is the place for great barbeque and a fun place to hang out!

If you plan to visit the Original Famous Dave's in beautiful Hayward, WI, bring your camera. This restaurant is probably the most-photographed restaurant in all of Wisconsin!

137

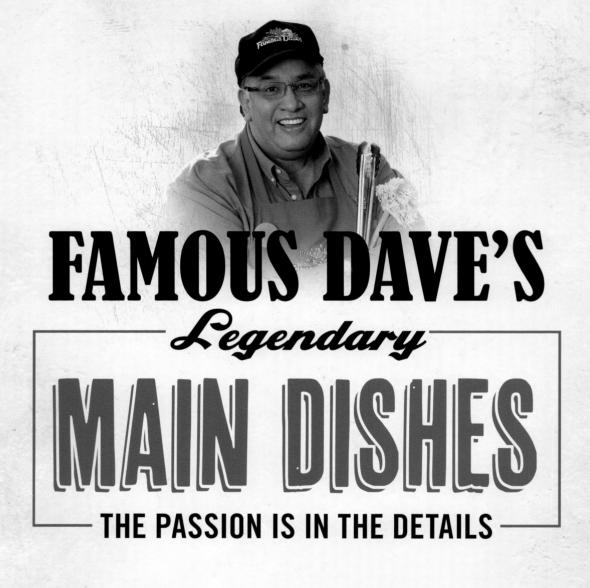

# FAMOUS DAVE'S
## *Legendary*
# MAIN DISHES
### THE PASSION IS IN THE DETAILS

# EAT ★ LAUGH ★ PARTY

# TABLE OF CONTENTS

# CHAR-GRILLED FAJITAS!

**This is FUN food! Tex-Mex Fajitas done on the grill.** Tasty strips of top sirloin make this recipe quick and easy. Traditionally, skirt or flank steaks are used in fajitas because these beef cuts are inexpensive. However, those cuts are so tough you need to marinate the steaks to make them tender and flavorful. I use top sirloin which is less work and a more tender cut. These steak fajitas are a festival of flavors served with grilled onions, colorful bell peppers, slices of avocados and toppings of robust salsa, and my tasty **Festive Party Guacamole** (pg. 56).

---

### Delightfully serves a party of 4

2 lbs. top sirloin steak

2 Tbsp. Steak Seasoning (pg. 143)

2 tsp. Aleppo chili pepper

2 tsp. cumin

light olive oil

2 green bell peppers, sliced into strips

2 red bell peppers, sliced into strips

2 yellow bell peppers, sliced into strips

2 large red onions, sliced into strips

kosher salt

fresh ground black pepper

3 limes

1 package of good quality 10" flour tortillas

2 avocados, sliced

1 cup salsa

1 cup sour cream

Festive Party Guacamole (pg. 56)

At least 2 hours before you are ready to grill, marinate your steak. Mix steak seasoning, Aleppo chili pepper, and cumin. Generously sprinkle chili-flavored steak seasoning over steaks, reserve 2 teaspoons of seasoning. Let sit for 30 minutes. Sprinkle olive oil over the steaks and make sure both sides are well covered. Refrigerate for 2 hours.

Prepare the peppers and onions. Just before you begin to grill, lightly toss veggies in olive oil. Sprinkle with salt and pepper.

Prepare your grill and place a veggie grilling pan on the grill to heat up. Remove steaks from the marinade and gently shake off excess olive oil. Next, place steaks on grill. Using tongs, place the veggies into the hot grill pan. Be careful not to have too much oil on the veggies and steaks or they will flare up.

Sear the steaks for about 4 minutes on each side; this recipe is best with medium-rare steaks. When veggies start to caramelize, remove from grilling pan and prepare them to serve.

While letting steaks rest for a few minutes… slightly warm tortillas on grill. Don't over-grill the tortillas or they will dry out and tear while you try to wrap your fajitas. Place tortillas under a dishtowel to keep warm.

Slice the steaks into thin strips against the grain, spritz with fresh lime juice and dust with chili-flavored steak seasoning. Serve with grilled veggies, slices of avocado, salsa, sour cream, **Festive Party Guacamole** (pg. 56), and limes.

**Yields:** 8 good-sized fajitas.

# MAN BAIT Bone-In Ribeye
## Dressed with Dave's Secret Bourbon Steak Sauce

**For some special backyard parties, the only worthy food is... steaks on the grill.** I love a tender, juicy, bone-in ribeye quickly charred over an open grill. Everything starts with a great cut of meat. When cooking for my family, I select a thicker 2" steak...but for parties, I found a 12 to 14 oz., 1-1/4" thick, steak is plenty and easier to grill when you have a lot of hungry mouths to feed. Next, you need a great steak seasoning... after that, a great flavorful steak does not need anything. However, if you want a mouth-watering treat, then you'll fall in love with **Dave's Secret Bourbon Steak Sauce**. The ingredients to this magical potion have been requested over the years but flatly denied until now!

## Dave's Special Blend Steak Seasoning

2 Tbsp. Famous Dave's Steak and Burger Seasoning

2 Tbsp. minced garlic chips*

2 Tbsp. kosher salt

1 Tbsp. fresh fine ground black pepper

1 Tbsp. fresh table ground black pepper

1 Tbsp. Spice Islands Old Hickory Smoked Salt

2 tsp. Accent (optional but recommended!)

**Mix all the seasonings in a small bowl. Store in an airtight container until needed.**

**\*Grind minced garlic chips in a coffee grinder for the best flavor.**

## Dave's Secret Bourbon Steak Sauce

1/2 cup Famous Dave's Texas Pit BBQ Sauce

1/4 cup Lea & Perrins Thick Classic Worcestershire Sauce

2 Tbsp. B-V Beef Broth and Sauce Concentrate

2 Tbsp. sweet chili sauce

1 shot of Jack Daniel's Tennessee Whiskey

**Mix all ingredients in a medium bowl. Store in an airtight container until needed.**

Delightfully serves a party of 4

4 bone-in ribeye steaks

Dave's Special Blend Steak Seasoning

4 Tbsp. melted butter

Dave's Secret Bourbon Steak Sauce

vegetable oil

**Generously shake Dave's Special Blend Steak Seasoning over your steaks one hour before you are ready to grill. Start a good wood fire or light your charcoal; get your coals good and hot so the grill grates are ready. Soak a cloth with quality vegetable oil, and then use tongs to rub down the grill grates right before placing your steaks on the grill. Do not use olive oil.**

**Place steaks on the grill. You may turn your steaks to create diamond marks, but you only want to flip your steaks once. Flip the steaks quickly and carefully douse each steak with a tablespoon of melted butter; be prepared for a major flare-up! ONLY DO THIS OUTSIDE! This flare-up will give the steaks a nice char while keeping them Rare or Medium Rare inside. Once the flare-up starts to subside, the steaks should be done. Remove immediately. Serve with Dave's Secret Bourbon Steak Sauce on the side.**

## Famous Dave's Hot Tips!

Always talk to the butcher the day before and request your steaks to be cut especially for you on the date of your party. Treat your butcher like one of the family and you'll always be provided with great cuts of meat!

Another tip for great steaks… do NOT trim off the fat. The fat will render off onto the hot coals causing flare ups, which add more flavor.

THE ONLY THING JUICIER THAN MY CHICKEN IS SOME GOOD GOSSIP!

# Smoky Rotisserie Chicken on the Grill

**Once you master the art of rotisserie chicken...you'll never want to cook any other way.** I absolutely love making this chicken because the revolving rotisserie bastes the chicken in its own juices, plus the smoky aroma of smoldering coals combines in a magical way to make this the best-tasting chicken ever. Yes, it may take extra time to marinaee the chicken and prepare your grill, but the juicy, moist, flavorful chicken it creates makes this recipe worth your while!

---

## Delightfully serves a party of 6

**2 roasting chickens**

**1 Tbsp. kosher salt**

**1 Tbsp. canning salt**

**2 Tbsp. Knorr or Maggi Chicken Soup Base** (dry granulated)

**2 Tbsp. lemon pepper**

**2 Tbsp. ground Aleppo chili pepper**

**1 Tbsp. dry sweet basil** (crush in hand to release flavor)

**1 Tbsp. sweet paprika**

**1 Tbsp. ground dry rosemary** (grind in coffee grinder)

**1 Tbsp. ground cumin**

**1 Tbsp. granulated garlic**

**1 Tbsp. granulated onion**

**1 Tbsp. fresh ground black pepper**

**1 tsp. Accent** (optional)

**2 tsp. Spice Islands Hickory Smoke Salt** (optional)

**1/2 cup purified water**

**1 Tbsp. fresh lemon juice**

**3 Tbsp. olive oil**

Depending on how much time you have to prepare, I created two seasoning preparation methods: Quick & Easy Dry Sprinkle and Marinade Paste.

**Quick & Easy Dry Sprinkle Preparation:** Used when you need to roast a chicken quickly without hours for marinating. Mix all the dry seasonings together in a bowl. Spread olive oil on the chickens and generously sprinkle with seasoning. Roast or grill. This dry seasoning can be stored in an airtight container for months.

**Marinade Paste Preparation:** Used for a more robust flavor when you have the time to marinate your chickens. In a bowl, mix the water and the lemon juice together. Add the dry seasonings. Mix thoroughly. Do NOT add the oil. Let the wet seasonings rest for one hour so the seasonings can bloom and combine flavors.

After one hour, add olive oil and thoroughly mix.

Generously rub seasoning over chickens. Place in a plastic bag and refrigerate for a minimum of 4 hours. Remove the chickens from refrigerator, and let sit for 1/2 hour to remove the chill from the chickens before placing on the grill. This seasoning can be held for up to two weeks, refrigerated in an airtight container.

### Grilling the Chickens

Prepare the grill by igniting a full charcoal chimney, and placing the glowing coals in the middle of your grill. With a small metal shovel, push the charcoal to the perimeter of the grill leaving enough space for an aluminum pan. In the pan, place about 2 inches of water, which will catch the juices from the chickens. It's important to use water in the pan, otherwise the wonderful tasty juices dripping from the chickens will evaporate and burn.

Place the chickens on the rotisserie and begin grilling. Chickens will take about 1-1/2 hours to fully cook. After 1 hour, check the temperature of the chickens, then start watching your chickens to achieve the proper temperature. You don't want them to overcook and dry out.

Remove chickens when the internal temperature reaches 160 to 165 degrees or when their juices run clear. Allow the chickens to rest for 15 minutes before carving. Remove the drip pan from the grill. Most of the water will have evaporated from the pan, leaving tasty drippings, which can be splashed over the carved chicken. This will give you a wonderful, juicy, tasty rotisserie chicken.

# Hawaiian BBQ Party Chicken

**If your chicken is starting to taste like chicken...this smoky Hawaiian "rotisserie" chicken will jumpstart your taste buds!** Juicy rotisserie chicken slathered with a lip-smackin' Hawaiian BBQ & Basting Sauce is guaranteed to put the sway back in your grass skirt! It's sure to be one of your family's favorite BBQ party recipes!

**Delightfully serves a party of 4**

**2 Roasting Chickens**

**Hawaiian Chicken Seasoning**

2 Tbsp. cumin

3 Tbsp. table salt

2 Tbsp. chili powder

2 Tbsp. sweet paprika

2 Tbsp. granulated garlic powder

2 Tbsp. granulated onion powder

1 Tbsp. ground celery

2 Tbsp. Knorr Chicken Base, Sam's Club Brand or Maggi Chicken Soup

1 Tbsp. fresh ground black pepper

2 tsp. cayenne

1 tsp. Accent (optional)

3/4 cup water (must add water to lemon first)

3 Tbsp. lemon juice

1/4 cup light olive or canola oil

grilled pineapple slices

**Hawaiian BBQ Chicken Seasoning** (will season 2 chickens)

In a bowl, mix dry ingredients first. Add water & lemon juice slowly while mixing to avoid clumping. It's important that this mixture is thoroughly mixed before adding olive oil. Add olive oil last and mix well.

**Preparing Chickens**

Generously rub seasoning over the chickens. Place chickens in a plastic bag and refrigerate for 4 hours. Remove the chickens from the regrigerator, and let sit for 30 minutes before placing on the grill.

Prepare **Hawaiian BBQ & Basting Sauce**; set aside.

Ideally, this chicken should be cooked on a charcoal grill outfitted with a rotisserie. It's incredible "smokiness" and taste intensifies as it rotisseries over smoldering coals. Once the chicken is almost done roasting and has reached an internal temperature of 165°, begin basting with sauce. Baste the chicken, continue to grill until the sauce begins to caramelize then baste again; repeat three times. This process will only take a few minutes. The chicken should be crispy and almost "burnt" or charred… the real flavor comes from charring the sauce and crisping up the skin. Allow chickens to rest for 15 minutes before carving.

Oven Prep: If you absolutely must… preheat oven to 350 degrees and bake about 45 minutes. Once the chicken is almost done roasting and reaches an internal temperature of 165°, begin basting with sauce. Baste the chicken and put back in the oven, continue roasting until the sauce begins to caramelize, pull out and baste again; repeat three times. This process will only take a few minutes. You must finish off the chicken in the broiler; set broiler on high to caramelize the sauce, giving it a flavor like it was flamed on a spit over a live fire. Allow chickens to rest for 15 minutes before carving.

Serve with grilled pineapple slices.

# Hawaiian BBQ & Basting Sauce

1/4 cup ketchup

1/4 cup soy sauce

1/2 cup light brown sugar

1/4 cup clover honey

2 Tbsp. fresh ginger, finely grated

2 tsp. fresh garlic, finely minced and crushed

1/4 cup fresh lime juice

1/4 cup Mizkan Nakano Original Seasoned Rice Vinegar

2 Tbsp. Asian sweet chili sauce

2 tsp. Sambal Oelek chili paste

2 tsp. Sriracha hot chili sauce

1/2 tsp. sesame seed oil

1/4 cup light olive or canola oil

Mix all ingredients together. For best results, hold overnight so all the flavors can bloom into their full strength.

This recipe must be put together using the EXACT products as listed for the best flavor profile.

For thicker sauce:

Mix soy sauce, lime juice, and rice vinegar together. Remove 3 tablespoons of liquid and to this add 2 tablespoons of corn starch; mix well. Add mix back to the main recipe. Bring to boil in a sauce pan until cornstarch has firmed up the sauce.

This Hawaiian BBQ Chicken is so tasty… it will put the SWAY back into your grass skirt!

HEAD FOR THE ISLANDS, where the sun sets and the FUN begins. You're going to love this recipe... it's Shrimply Delicious!

# BBQ Shrimp with Mango Salsa

**This is one of my personal favorite recipes...** delicious, citrus-infused shrimp, grilled and served over a delightful tropical Mango Salsa. It's the perfect light entrée for any backyard get-together.

---

**Delightfully serves a party of 5**

### SHRIMP

**2 lbs. (16-20) raw shrimp, peeled and deveined**

**Dave's All-Purpose Fish Seasoning** (pg. 173)

**Famous Dave's Sweet & Zesty BBQ Sauce**

**fresh limes**

### MARINADE

**1 cup Famous Dave's Sweet & Zesty BBQ Sauce**

**1/4 cup light olive oil**

**1 cup pineapple juice**

**1/4 cup pineapple juice concentrate**

**1/2 cup lime juice**

**1 Tbsp. Sriracha hot chili sauce**

Peel and devein shrimp; place in a large plastic bag.

Prepare marinade. In a bowl, mix BBQ sauce, olive oil, pineapple juice, pineapple concentrate, lime juice, and chili sauce together. Pour marinade into plastic bag with shrimp, seal and refrigerate for at least 2 hours. After 2 hours, drain shrimp into a sieve over a bowl, and discard the marinade.

Skewer shrimp with metal skewers or wooden skewers soaked in water. Lightly season shrimp with **Dave's All-Purpose Fish Seasoning** and spray with a non-stick cooking spray. Grill shrimp; depending on the temperature of your grill it won't take long to the grill shrimp, once they start looking opaque they are done. Baste with straight Sweet & Zesty BBQ Sauce just before taking off the grill; okay! enough to caramelize the sauce.

Arrange **Mango Salsa** in the center of a large platter and place BBQ shrimp on top. Take a few lime slices and spritz lime juice over the shrimp. Garnish the edge of your platter with lime wedges.

## Mango Salsa

---

**1 cup of mandarin oranges, chopped, drained** (reserve syrup)

**2 tsp. Ball Fruit-Fresh Produce Protector**

**1 cup fresh pineapple, chopped** (reserve juice)

**2 shot glasses of Grand Marnier**

**1 cup of mango, chopped**

**1 cup red bell pepper, chopped**

**1 cup red onion, chopped**

**2 jalapeños, diced**

**3 cloves garlic, minced**

**1 tsp. kosher salt**

**1 cup of avocado, chopped**

Drain mandarin oranges, rough chop and reserve 1/2 cup of packing syrup. Add Ball Fruit-Fresh Produce Protector to mandarin orange syrup and mix well.

After coring pineapple, reserve the juice. Add 1/2 cup of pineapple juice to mandarin orange juice. Add Grand Marnier to this mix and set aside.

In a large bowl, add mangos, mandarin oranges, pineapple, red bell peppers, red onion, jalapeños, garlic, and kosher salt and gently toss to mix. Set mango mixture aside.

Chop avocados, add to mandarin orange mix and set aside.

Add the avocado mixture to the mango mixture and gently fold... be careful not to smash the avocados. Serve immediately.

# BACON-WRAPPED PORK LOIN

**Wrap anything in bacon and you've just transported yourself into Hog Heaven!** I encourage you not to bypass this recipe because it looks complicated…it is easier than it looks and the results are so awesome you'll be glad you gave this recipe a try. Smoky meats don't get more mouth-wateringly tender and juicy than a center-cut loin, stuffed with juicy peaches and apples, wrapped in hickory-smoked bacon, and smoked over smoldering hickory and apple wood. This is a tasty treat that's worth the extra effort especially if you want to knock the socks off of your family & friends with your Pitmaster skills.

A Pork-aholic's Dream!

**Delightfully serves a party of 6**

4 pork tenderloins

1 cup Dave's Honey Mustard Slathering Sauce

kosher salt & fresh ground black pepper to taste

4 apples

4 fresh peaches (frozen or canned will NOT work!)

1 cup golden raisins

4 lbs. hickory-smoked bacon (not thick slice, 1 pound of bacon for each pork tenderloin bacon weave)

Drunken Apricot BBQ Sauce (pg. 58)

**Variations:** If you like your smoked pork a little bit sweeter, you can sprinkle the top of the bacon weave with brown sugar before smoking. I have also used maple which works nicely with the smokiness.

Sometimes I place a few slices of garlic cloves and a sprig of rosemary between the pork and the bacon weave depending on what I am stuffing the loin with. This works great when I stuff the loins with savory cooked wild rice, goat cheese, sunflower seeds, celery, and onions.

## DAVE'S HONEY MUSTARD SLATHERING SAUCE

1 cup mayonnaise

1/4 cup yellow mustard

1/4 cup Dijon mustard

1/2 cup 100% clover honey (no fructose added)

1 Tbsp. stone-ground mustard

1/4 tsp. salt

1/4 tsp. white pepper

1/4 tsp. cayenne pepper

1/4 tsp. paprika

1/2 tsp. citric acid

Mix all ingredients together. Refrigerate until needed.

Dress tenderloin by removing silver skin and fat. Slather with honey mustard sauce and marinate overnight. After marinating, using a paper towel, wipe loins clean of any excess honey mustard. Next, slice the tenderloin lengthwise to butterfly. Cover with plastic wrap and lightly pound to even out the meat. You are only pounding it to even out, NOT to pound it thin!

Spread pork tenderloin flat and season with salt and pepper. In the center of the flat tenderloin, layer apple slices, peach slices, and 1/4 cup golden raisins. Gently roll meat up into a log and pinch to close the ends off; set aside.

On a large piece of butcher or freezer paper, take one pound of bacon and weave a square. Next, take the stuffed tenderloin log and place it on the woven bacon. Carefully fold over one end of the woven bacon and roll up. Repeat with other tenderloin logs.

Place bacon-wrapped pork loin in the smoker. Smoke over indirect heat at 350 degrees with hickory and apple wood. Smoke until the bacon turns brown and the internal temperature of the pork reaches 145° degrees. Let the meat rest before slicing. Serve with **Drunken Apricot BBQ Sauce** (pg. 58), or mix in some leftover **Dave's Honey Mustard Slathering Sauce** for some extra robust flavors!

# Bluehorse Maple Chops
## WITH FRESH MANDARIN APPLESLAW

**This will put the Giddy-Up back into your chops!** Everyone always wonders how I get such hearty flavors from my pork… it's two things: a good smoky fire and a great-tasting marinade! There isn't a better all-around marinade than this one… pure maple syrup which sings with wood smoke, a good fresh-grated horseradish, blue agave honey, and stone-ground mustard, all jacked-up with Sriarcha. These mouthwatering chops are paired with fresh chilled apples & mandarin oranges in a refreshing new take on appleslaw.

## Delightfully serves a party of 4

**4 thick pork chops**

**50/50 blend of kosher salt & fresh coarse ground black pepper**

**Bluehorse Maple Marinade**

### Bluehorse Maple Marinade

**1/4 cup pure maple syrup**

**1/4 cup blue agave honey**

**2 Tbsp. fresh ground horseradish**

**2 Tbsp. stone ground mustard**

**1/4 cup apple cider vinegar**

**1 Tbsp. fresh garlic, minced & smashed**

**2 tsp. Sriracha sauce**

**2 tsp. kosher salt**

In a large bowl, mix all ingredients for Bluehorse Maple Marinade. Place pork chops in marinade; cover and refrigerate overnight or at least 4 hours.

Remove pork chops from refrigerator; sprinkle with salt and pepper.

Prepare grill with charcoal and a small hickory log. Smoke chops by indirect heat over low smoldering coals & smoking hickory log for about 20 minutes. Open the grill and let the log catch on fire, then quickly give the chops a sear while basting with marinade. Chops are done when they reach an internal temperature of 145 degrees.

Serve with **Mandarin Appleslaw**.

*My favorite appleslaw recipe!*
## MANDARIN APPLESLAW

**8 chilled apples, cored and peeled**

**2 cups chilled mandarin oranges + 1/2 cup of juice**

**1 Tbsp. Ball Fruit-Fresh Produce Protector**

Core and peel 8 chilled apples. Place in a food processor and pulse briefly to turn into a coarse pulp. DO NOT over pulse and turn apples into a mush... you want apples to be rough-chopped, like a coleslaw.

In a medium bowl, add 1/2 cup of mandarin orange juice and 1 tablespoon of Ball Fruit-Fresh Produce Protector. Mix well and then add appleslaw. Next rough chop mandarin oranges and add to appleslaw. Cover and refrigerate at least 1 hour.

**Yields:** about 4 cups of appleslaw.

**MMmmm**...juicy, tender, smoky– you'll be lickin' your chops!

# SPICY ORANGE & TERIYAKI BEEF KABOBS

**Bundles of BBQ Happiness!** I love kabobs. I think kabobs are an awesome party food that makes serving a lot of people quick and easy. There a number of recipes that call for beef tenderloin, which is great if you have a bulging pocketbook but not necessary for a tasty steak. Top sirloin is just as tasty—especially marinated and served medium rare. This is a five-star recipe featuring sirloin swaddled in bacon, layered between fresh pineapple, red onion, and red and green bell peppers.

---

## Delightfully serves a party of 6

2 lbs. boneless beef sirloin

kosher salt & fresh ground black pepper to taste

Orange Teriyaki Sauce

1 lb. hickory-smoked bacon

1 fresh pineapple

1 large red onion

2 red bell peppers

2 green bell peppers

Day Ahead - Cut sirloin steak into 1-1/2 inch cubes (about 2 to 3 ounces each). Salt & pepper. Wrap in butcher paper, and put back into refrigerator.

Prepare the **Orange Teriyaki Sauce**. Once cool, divide marinade in half. In a glass or plastic container, place half of the marinade with the steak cubes and marinate overnight in refrigerator. Refrigerate remaining marinade.

Next day, prepare charcoal grill. Remove steaks and reserved sauce from refrigerator. Wipe excess marinade off steak cubes. Wrap a 1/2 slice of bacon around each steak cube. Chop pineapple, peppers, and onion into large pieces. Skewer bacon-wrapped steak cube, red onion, pineapple, red and green bell peppers; repeat layers until skewer is full.

Grill 4-5 minutes on each side, depending on how well you like your meat done. Baste skewers with reserved sauce just before removing from grill.

## ORANGE TERIYAKI SAUCE

1/4 cup ketchup

1/4 cup teriyaki sauce

1/2 cup orange juice concentrate

1/2 cup dark brown sugar

2 Tbsp. fresh finely grated ginger

1 Tbsp. fresh finely minced and crushed garlic

1/4 cup fresh lemon juice

1/4 cup Mizkan Nakano Original Seasoned Rice Vinegar

2 Tbsp. Asian sweet chili sauce

2 tsp. Sambal Oelek chili paste

2 tsp. Sriracha hot chili sauce

1 tsp. sesame seed oil

2 Tbsp. cornstarch

1/2 cup Famous Dave's Sweet & Zesty BBQ Sauce

*Use aluminum foil to protect the wooden skewers.*

Mix all ingredients except cornstarch and BBQ sauce in sauce pan. Mix in cornstarch and bring to a boil. Boil for one minute and remove pan from heat. Stir in BBQ sauce. Cool to room temperature.

# TASTY WHITE CHICKEN THIGHS

**I love these beer-marinated chicken thighs served up with a tasty White Barbecue Sauce… especially for large parties.** The chicken thighs are juicy and flavorful but the key is their uniformity in size, which makes them easy to grill. This Alabama favorite is a great new taste for chicken… it's creamy, tangy, spicy, and cool… perfect for a summer barbecue. My good friend Chris Lilly of Big Bob Gibson's in Decatur, Alabama, has made this white barbecue sauce famous all over the country. Now you can enjoy this Southern delicacy too!

**Delightfully serves a party of 6**

**10 skin-on, bone-in chicken thighs** (about 3 lb.)

## BEER BRINE

**4 cups Samuel Adams or a good full-body lager**

**1/2 cup apple juice concentrate**

**2 Tbsp. kosher salt**

**1 cup onion, chopped**

## CHICKEN SEASONING

**1 Tbsp. kosher salt**

**1 Tbsp. canning salt**

**2 Tbsp. Maggi or Knorr Chicken Flavor Bouillon granules**

**1 Tbsp. lemon pepper**

**1 Tbsp. dried thyme**

**1 Tbsp. dried rosemary** (ground in coffee grinder)

**1 Tbsp. ground cumin**

**1 Tbsp. paprika**

**1 Tbsp. granulated garlic**

**1 Tbsp. granulated onion powder**

**1 tsp. fresh ground black pepper**

Prepare **White Barbecue Sauce** the night before.

Prepare beer brine and place in a plastic tub. Place chicken thighs in brine, cover and refrigerate at least 4 hours, but not overnight. You want a noticeable hint of the beer brine; if you marinate the chicken too long it will overpower the sauce. Remove the chicken thighs from the brine, pat dry. Remove **White Barbecue Sauce** from the refrigerator.

Prepare grill with a full chimney starter of charcoal. Place hickory chunks in loosely wrapped foil and place near hot charcoal.

Next, prepare the chicken seasoning. In a bowl, combine all the ingredients and mix. Sprinkle the seasoning over the top and bottom of the marinated chicken thighs.

Place the thighs, meat side down, on a smoky grill and cook over indirect heat. Manage the thighs so they are fully cooked by continually moving them near the heat and away from the heat so that they don't get too overly burnt. Some char is fine for flavor. Turn over the thighs and place them skin side down and directly over the charcoal to flame kiss the skin. The grilling process should take about 30 minutes… or until the juices run clear.

After grilling, dunk your thighs into the sauce, plate, and serve. Serve with **White Barbecue Sauce** on the side.

## WHITE BARBECUE SAUCE

**2 cups mayonnaise**

**3/4 cup white vinegar**

**3/4 cup apple juice concentrate**

**1 Tbsp. fresh lemon juice**

**1 Tbsp. ranch dressing dry mix**

**1 Tbsp. sugar**

**1-1/2 tsp. salt**

**1 Tbsp. fresh ground black pepper**

**2 tsp. stone-ground mustard**

**2 cloves garlic, minced in a garlic press**

**1 tsp. coarse ground hot horseradish**

**1 tsp. Louisiana hot sauce**

**1 tsp. liquid hickory smoke**

In a large bowl, combine all the ingredients. Mix well, cover, and refrigerate overnight.

# Raspberry Agave Chicken

**You'll never disappoint your family or guests with this colorful, tasty chicken.** This is one of my personal favorites! Smoky, grilled chicken draped with a colorful tasty raspberry sauce.

---

### Delightfully serves a party of 4

4 boneless, skinless, chicken breast halves

2 Tbsp. kosher salt

1 Tbsp. fresh coarse ground black pepper

Prepare **Raspberry Marinade**. Add chicken breasts and raspberry marinade to a plastic bag and marinate in the refrigerator for at least 4 hours turning several times to distribute marinade.

Prepare charcoal grill. Remove chicken and wipe off excess marinade. Mix kosher salt with fresh coarse ground black pepper and lightly season chicken. Place on grill. Grill chicken until internal temperature reaches 165° degrees or juices run clear. While grilling, prepare **Raspberry Agave Sauce**. Spoon sauce over chicken and serve.

### RASPBERRY MARINADE

10 oz. package frozen raspberries in syrup (reserve syrup)

1 cup Wish Bone Robusto Italian Dressing

Thaw raspberries, drain and separate juice and berries. Reserve raspberry syrup for the **Raspberry Agave Sauce**. Place berries in a large resealable plastic bag and add Italian dressing.

### RASPBERRY AGAVE SAUCE

2 Tbsp. butter

1/4 cup sweet onion, finely diced

reserved raspberry syrup (from marinade)

2 Tbsp. blue agave honey

1 tsp. kosher salt

1/4 tsp. white pepper

1/2 cup Girard's Raspberry Dressing

1 cup fresh raspberries

1/4 cup heavy cream

In a sauté pan, melt butter and sauté onions until tender. Add reserved syrup from frozen raspberries, honey, salt, and white pepper, bring to a rolling simmer. Add raspberry dressing and raspberries; return to simmer while occasionally stirring. Add heavy cream and return to simmer.

Continue cooking while stirring, until the sauce reduces to the right thickness. Remove from heat. If you don't want the seeds, strain sauce before serving.

# PIZZA ON THE GRILL

**After barbecue, my first food love is homemade pizza on the grill.** You get all the smokiness from real smoldering coals and a high heat you can't get from your indoor oven. High heat makes the best crunchy crust and the flavor is unbeatable.

Pizza on the grill is great for parties... the cooking time is a quick 5 minutes compared to 15 minutes in the oven. Pizza on the grill is every bit as tasty as the big and fancy wood-fired pizza ovens, but without the hassle and expense of having a wood-fired pizza oven. Impress your family and friends by turning your backyard grill into the best pizzeria in town!

**Delightfully serves a party of 6**

## PIZZA DOUGH

**This recipe makes 3 - 12" or 14" pizzas depending how thin you roll your dough**

**1 cup lukewarm water** (115 to 120 degrees)

**2 Tbsp. olive oil**

**3 cups all-purpose flour**

**1 package Red Star Platinum Baking Yeast**

**1 tsp. salt**

**1 tsp. sugar**

Add the oil to the water. Next, mix all the dry ingredients together, then add the water & oil. Mix together by hand until everything comes together.

Place the dough into a stand mixer with a dough hook. Knead for 2 to 3 minutes. Empty the dough out onto a lightly floured kneading surface and knead for a quick minute to bring the dough together. Place into a well-oiled bowl, rolling the dough around until it becomes covered in oil. Place a damp towel over the dough and let rise for one hour.

After one hour, punch dough down and divide into three balls. If you refrigerate overnight, make sure you bring the dough to room temperature before using.

## Famous Dave's Hot Tip:

One of my new discoveries is Red Star Platinum Baking Yeast with Dough Enhancers! It makes a great pizza dough that's easy to work with... you don't need fancy pizza flours with this yeast to get a good flavorful, crunchy pizza crust. I usually double the recipe and hold my dough 3 days in the refrigerator; the yeast continues to create great crusty flavors overnight. Fleischmann's Pizza Crust Yeast is another great yeast for pizza dough.

## PREPARING THE GRILL

The key to successful pizza on the grill is to get a good pile of charcoal going with the pizza stone on top, so that the stone heats up with the charcoal. If you put a cold stone over hot coals it may crack. This next step is important... once the coals are glowing hot, carefully lift the grill grate and stone out of the grill and place it somewhere so it won't burn anything while you fix the coals. Next, with a small metal shovel, push the coals out of the middle and pile them up along the outside edge of the grill. Put the pizza stone back on the grill and close the lid to let the pizza stone get hot again.

You don't want the red-hot coals directly underneath the pizza stone or your dough will burn before the ingredients on top get hot and the cheese melts. By pushing the hot coals to the outside you also allow the intense heat to rise up into the upper part of the grill chamber, which quickly cooks the top of your pizza.

**CAUTION:** If you place the pizza directly on the grill it can get too hot and quickly burn the underside before the top finishes cooking. If you don't use a pizza stone, let the coals burn down so the heat isn't as intense. Don't worry about putting the pizza directly on the grill grates... your pizza will not fall through. Be careful when removing the pizza from the grill, so it doesn't stick to the grates and tear your pizza. Best advice... buy the grill pizza stone by Weber and you'll appreciate years of great-tasting pizza on the grill.

DAVE'S PIZZA OVEN!

After barbecue, my first food love is homemade pizza on the grill.

# BARBECUE PIZZA

Your dough is made and your grill is heating up, time to make the pizza! Most folks are familiar with regular Italian-style pizza, but once they taste a BBQ Pizza made on the grill… they get hooked on the tasty flavors of smoky barbecue on a pizza! The following ingredients are just a start. Discover your own tasty combinations using other ingredients. Try making my **Traditional Chicago-Style Thin Crust Pizza** (pg. 163) or create your own Hawaiian or Teriyaki Pizzas.

The following ingredients make three BBQ pizzas.

**1 lb. twice-smoked beef sausage or smoked kielbasa**

**3 lb. rotisserie chicken, hand shredded into chunks**

**corn meal**

**20 oz. Famous Dave's Rich & Sassy BBQ Sauce**

**3 Roma tomatoes, rough chopped**

**1 lb. fresh mozzarella, sliced into 1/4-inch slices**

**1 pint mushrooms, sliced**

**2 or 3 jalapeños, sliced** (optional)

**1 lb. sharp cheddar cheese, shredded** (can also be smoked)

While your grill is getting hot, twice smoke your sausage until it gets a nice smoky char. Slice into 1/2-inch pieces and set aside. Try Andouille or Chorizo sausage for added excitement!

Hand shred a rotisserie chicken and set aside.

Prepare dough into a 12" or 14" round pizza. Don't fret if it isn't perfectly round, I think the odd shapes add to the "artisan" hand-crafted appeal. On a pizza peel, spread a handful of corn meal and place the pizza dough on top.

Next, ladle about 1/4 cup of BBQ sauce on your pizza; push the sauce around onto the dough until the entire pizza is equally covered. You don't need a lot of sauce on a pizza.

Spread the rough-chopped tomatoes around. Add mozzarella. Add the chicken, smoked sausage, mushrooms, and jalapeños. Top with shredded cheddar cheese.

Check to make sure your pizza will easily slide off your peel. Otherwise, when you go to slide it off your peel onto the pizza stone, the dough will stick and all your ingredients will go flying off the dough onto the hot pizza stone. Once your pizza is safely on the pizza stone, cover the grill.

Check pizza in five minutes… it should be done. Enjoy!

## MMmmm...
### Barbecue Pizza!

# TRADITIONAL CHICAGO-STYLE THIN CRUST PIZZA

pizza dough (pg. 161)

Dave's Robust Pizza Sauce (pg. 164)

Dave's Italian Sausage (pg. 164)

1-1/2 cups mozzarella cheese

1/2 lb. mushrooms, sliced

1 green pepper, sliced

1/2 cup black olives, sliced

corn meal

Prepare **Dave's Robust Pizza Sauce** (pg. 164) and **Dave's Italian Sausage** (pg. 164) one day ahead.

Prepare your **Pizza Dough** (pg. 161). Prepare your pizza grill (pg. 161 for directions). Prepare dough into a 12" or 14" round pizza. Don't fret if it isn't perfectly round, I think the odd shapes add to the "artisan" hand-crafted appeal.

On a pizza peel, spread a handful of corn meal and place the pizza dough on top. Next, ladle about 1/4 cup of pizza sauce onto your pizza; push the sauce around on the dough until the entire pizza is equally covered. You don't need a lot of sauce on a pizza.

Next, add 1 to 1-1/2 cups of mozzarella to lightly cover your pizza. If you want a heavy cheese pizza then add more, but light on the cheese works better.

Next, add quarter-size pinches of sausage, mushrooms, green peppers, and black olives.

Check to make sure your pizza will easily slide off your peel. Otherwise, when you go to slide it off your peel onto the pizza stone, the dough will stick and all your ingredients will go flying off the dough onto the hot pizza stone. Once your pizza is safely on the pizza stone, cover the grill.

Check pizza in five minutes... it should be done. Enjoy!

Pizza Stone for the Grill

Chicago-Style Thin Crust Pizza

## DAVE'S ROBUST PIZZA SAUCE

2 cups Hunt's Tomato Paste

6 cups Hunt's Crushed Tomatoes

2 Tbsp. sugar

2 tsp. Morton's canning salt

2 tsp. fresh basil, finely minced and tightly packed

2 tsp. fresh thyme, finely minced and tightly packed

1 tsp. fresh oregano, finely minced and tightly packed

2 tsp. fennel seeds, finely ground in coffee grinder

1-1/2 tsp. black pepper, fresh ground in coffee grinder

1-1/2 tsp. crushed red pepper flakes

2 fresh garlic cloves, minced through a garlic press

In a bowl, mix tomato puree, crushed tomatoes, sugar, and sauce seasonings. Refrigerate until use. Ideally, sauce should be mixed one day before using to let the flavors fully blossom.

## DAVE'S ITALIAN SAUSAGE

1 lb. fresh ground pork

1 Tbsp. whole fennel seed

1 tsp. canning salt

1 tsp. sugar

1 tsp. fresh ground fennel seed

1 tsp. crushed red pepper flakes

1/2 tsp. fresh ground black pepper

1/4 tsp. fresh ground anise seed

1/4 tsp. granulated garlic

1/4 tsp. Accent

Mix all ingredients together. Place a plastic film directly over the sausage and hold overnight in the refrigerator to let all the flavors bloom. This sausage can be refrigerated in a tightly covered container for up to 5 days or should be frozen.

## IF YOU DON'T HAVE TIME— DAVE'S QUICK ITALIAN SAUSAGE

1 lb. fresh Johnsonville Hot Italian Sausage

1 lb. fresh Johnsonville Mild Italian Sausage

1 lb. Jimmy Dean's Regular Pork Sausage

3 Tbsp. whole fennel seeds

Mix all ingredients together and use. You may have leftover sausage, which you can freeze for later use.

**INCREDIBLY TASTY PIZZA LIKE THIS... WILL TURN YOUR BACKYARD GRILL INTO THE BEST PIZZA JOINT IN TOWN!**

# The WORLD'S BEST RIBS!
## Famous Dave's Killer BBQ Sticky Ribs

**Turn your backyard grill into the best rib joint in town with these mouthwatering BBQ babyback ribs.** These tender ribs are so tasty you'll never be able to host another party without your guests clamoring for these juicy apricot-glazed ribs. Make sure you have your best stretchy pants on and a mountain of napkins handy... it doesn't get any better than sweet corn, cold watermelon, hand-cut French fries, ice cold beer, and the best tasting ribs on the planet. Cold beer and tasty BBQ ribs are proof that God loves us and wants us to be happy!

165

water only saturated the wood to 1/8 inch.

**Delightfully serves a party of 6**

3 racks loin back ribs

1/2 cup melted hickory bacon grease

yellow mustard

BBQ Sticky Ribs Marinade

BBQ Sticky Ribs Rib Rub

BBQ Sticky Rib Frosting

## BBQ STICKY RIBS MARINADE

2 cans frozen apple juice concentrate

2 cans of purified water

4 Tbsp. canning salt (Morton's green box)

3 Tbsp. Wright's Liquid Smoke

4 Tbsp. Frank's Hot Sauce

Mix ingredients together. Equally divide the marinade into 4 two-gallon bags (turkey roasting bags work, too).

## BBQ STICKY RIBS RIB RUB

1/2 cup canning salt (Morton's green box)

1/3 cup light brown sugar

1/3 cup maple sugar

2 Tbsp. granulated onion powder

1 Tbsp. granulated garlic

1 Tbsp. paprika

1 Tbsp. fresh ground pepper

1 tsp. cayenne pepper

1 Tbsp. Accent (optional)

In a bowl, add all ingredients. Blend together.

## BBQ STICKY RIBS ~~SAUCE~~ FROSTING

2 cups Famous Dave's Rich & Sassy BBQ Sauce

2 cups Open Pit BBQ Sauce

1/2 cup dark brown sugar

12 oz. Smucker's Apricot Preserves

1/4 cup Frank's Hot Sauce

**PITMASTER TIP:** **Should you soak your wood in water before putting them on your charcoal?** It depends… if you are using wood chips, YES. Wood chips are small enough to absorb water, which prevents them from catching on fire and allows them to smolder and give off wonderful wood aromas. If you are using big wood chunks, which is what I recommend… then soaking does not help. If you soaked a big chunk of hardwood like hickory, oak, applewood, etc.,… overnight, you would find the water only saturated the wood to 1/8 inch. So after soaking all night, most of the wood is still bone dry. I recommend using big chucks of wood wrapped in foil just loose enough to let the smoke escape because the wood won't flare up or disappear like the smaller wood chips.

This BBQ Sauce is so incredibly delicious, it's like frosting for ribs!

166

# RIB-O-LICIOUS!

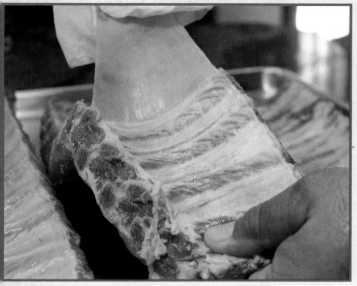

**1** Prepare loinbacks by pulling the membrane off the back of the ribs (bone side). Start on the small end of the rack and work your thumb under the membrane or use a butter knife. Once you have enough membrane to get a firm grip... grip the membrane with a paper towel and in one good pull, jerk the membrane off the rack.

**2** Prepare **BBQ Sticky Ribs Marinade**. Next, double up two kitchen plastic trash bags and place your ribs inside these bags meat side down. You should fit 2-3 racks per bag. You want to be careful the sharp ends of the bones don't puncture your bags.

**3** Pour your marinade over the ribs and securely tie up the bags to make them leakproof. Place on an aluminum pan and place in a refrigerator for 12 hours. At 7 hours, turn ribs over. After 12 hours, remove ribs from marinade and rinse them under cold water. Pat dry with paper towels.

**4** Rub both sides of ribs with a light coating of yellow mustard.

**5** Give your ribs a good even dusting with **BBQ Sticky Ribs Rib Rub** and let them set for one hour to let meat juices start mixing with seasonings. After the ribs have sat for one hour, drizzle the ribs with melted hickory bacon grease and place in smoker.

**6** Prepare your grill by igniting one charcoal chimney full of charcoal. Once glowing hot, pour charcoal towards one end of the grill as we will be placing the ribs opposite the heat. This is the "indirect heat" method of smoking. Next, add several large chunks of hickory, apple, or cherry wood. It's important you have plenty of smoldering chunks of smoking wood. You want a good billowing smoke wafting around in your grill.

**7** If your ribs don't fit bone side flat down on your grill, place them in a rib rack, heavy bone side down. Place this rib rack opposite of the heat. Smoke your ribs at 250 degrees for 2 hours.

**8** After two hours, remove ribs from the grill/smoker. Your ribs should have a beautiful mahogany color.

**9** Cover an aluminum pan with aluminum foil. Place ribs on the foil and generously brush ribs with **BBQ Sticky Ribs Frosting**. Pour 1/2 cup of water on bottom of pan. Next, create an aluminum tent over the ribs making sure the ribs do not touch the top of the foil. Bake for 1-1/2 to 2 hours at 300 degrees until the ribs are tender. Once the ribs are tender, remove them from the oven and keep covered until you are ready to caramelize the sauce on your ribs or your ribs will quickly lose their moisture and juiciness.

**DISCLAIMER:** Normally, I would be diametrically opposed to putting any rib in an oven. However, I realize not everyone has a true smoker and it is difficult to fix ribs for larger backyard parties because most charcoal grills cannot hold enough ribs. So, in this situation it makes sense to start the ribs on the grill and then tenderize them in the oven. Utilizing your grill and oven allows you to maximize smoking as many ribs as you can in your charcoal grill... I made my peace with the barbecue gods and they have mercifully forgiven me of this humbling barbeque "oven" transgression. But with all that being said... *these ribs are absolutely killer!!*

**10** While the ribs are baking, get your charcoal grill ready. The charcoal you used to smoke the ribs will have pretty much burned out by now. You will need to start a whole new chimney full of blazing hot charcoal, which you will pour into the center of your grill and spread out. You are not smoking, you are grilling this time. So your goal this time is to create a hot grill. Add extra coals if needed to build a bed of coals that covers the whole grill.

**11** Once your grill is hot, remove the foil from the ribs and quickly baste them with more sauce. Place the sauced ribs meat side down and baste the bone side with sauce. The grill is going to be very hot so move quickly; you might want to wear protective heat-resistant gloves. Use tongs to check your ribs. Once the sauce starts to caramelize, turn them over and slather the top side with more sauce. Repeat this process several times.

## Make sure the fingers you're lickin' are your own!

# You'd better be wearing your best stretchy pants!

**13** These ribs are so mouthwateringly delicious. I guarantee you will agree that these are the best "Tender as a mother's love" ribs you've ever tasted! In fact, make sure you tell all your party guests that they'd better be wearing their best stretchy pants!

**12** You are charring the sauce and building up layers of delicious flavors on your ribs. Don't over char your ribs or they will taste burnt… know the difference!!! When the ribs look beautifully caramelized, remove them from the grill. Slice into single bones and serve with extra sauce.

*"I believe man has a primal need to eat charred meat. There's something about chewing meat off a bone that brings out his inner caveman. This fascination of watching meat roast over an open fire is carried out today as millions of weekend barbeque warriors fire up their grills in conquest of the perfect charred piece of smoky meat! I, too, am a worshipper of the sacred flame!"*

~Famous Dave Anderson

There's nothing more American than a good ol' fashioned BBQ, good food, good music, plenty of cold beer, and lotsa friends!

# PITMASTER
## ★ BBQ LINGO ★

**Barbecue, Barbeque, Bar-B-Que, Bar-B-Q, BBQ, 'Que:** A purist's definition is meat smoked very slowly over low heat from smoldering hardwood coals until tender and may or may not be slathered with a barbeque sauce.

**HOWEVER**, to me… I never want to tell someone what they do in their backyard is NOT barbecue. So if you are having a good time with family and friends and you have hot dogs on a grill—that can be called a barbecue too!

**Barbeque Sauce:** The "Holy Grail" of barbeque… a liquid blend of spices, seasonings, fruit juices, sweeteners, and vegetables expertly combined to create a zesty flavorful sauce.

**Bark:** During the smoking process, sugars and spices in the rub join with the natural juices of the meat and carmelize in the heat and smoke to form a crunchy crust called the "bark" or "sugar cookie bark."

**Burnt Ends:** These are the crusty burnt edges of a smoked beef brisket or smoked pork that are trimmed off when taken out of the smoker. Highly prized for their crunchy concentration of flavors.

**Caramelizing:** The sugars in the rubs, fruit juices, BBQ sauce, and natural meat juices melt through the cooking or smoking process to form a crispy, crunchy, tasty crust on the meat.

**Marinade:** A liquid bath that meat or vegetables are soaked in for periods of time until the flavor of the marinade is imparted or infused into the meat or vegetable.

**Mop Sauce or Sop:** A liquid marinade or sauce that is applied like a baste during the cooking or smoking process.

**Smoke Ring:** A distinct reddish-pink ring that occurs naturally in the slow smoking process and is found around the top edges of the meat usually about ¼-inch deep.

**St. Louis Cut:** This is the center cut of the ribs right under the loinback ribs centered between the rib tips. This cut of ribs has good fat content marbling yielding great flavor when smoked.

**Rib Tips:** This is the bottom section of the spare rib. In the past, this section was generally considered "cast-off" and had no value. Inner-city BBQ joints smoked these "tips" and provided a cheap flavorful BBQ treat.

**Hot Links:** A flavorful sausage link infused with spices and fresh seasonings then smoked. The Hot Link is charred and may be slathered with a BBQ sauce.

**Rib Rub or Rub:** A dry blend of spices and seasonings applied to a meat before cooking or smoking.

**Shake:** A dry blend of seasonings that is "shaken" onto the meat or vegetables.

**Spare Ribs:** The whole slab of ribs including the brisket or rib tips found right under the loinback and lower on the belly of the hog.

**Grilling:** Direct cooking over high heat. The goal of grilling is to quickly sear and slightly char the meat to seal in the naturally flavorful juices.

**Smoking or Real Pit Barbequing:** Indirect heat is used to create slow smoky aromas that bathe the meat in a closed, contained space for long hours until the meat is tender and smoke infused.

**Fire Box:** An offset fire box container where live fire smolders and provides heat and smoke to a separate chamber that contains the meat. This is the indirect method of smoking.

**Pitmaster:** A devoted barbeque cook who has paid his dues tending a barbeque pit to become a master in how to build and manage the fire, smoke, and temperature.

**Rib Joint:** The affectionate name of a non-descript hole-in-the-wall storefront rib eatery that features real pit-smoked ribs and is usually passionately attended to by the owners.

# WILD ALASKAN CEDAR-PLANKED SALMON

**This is Mother Nature's most favorite recipe as there is not a more perfect combination than cedar, wild Alaskan salmon, maple syrup, and smokiness!** I personally guarantee you have never tasted a salmon so flavorful, moist, and pleasing to the palate. You can find clean cedar planks at most gourmet food stores, higher-end grocery stores, or online. Sourcing quality cedar planks to enjoy the best tasting salmon is worth the effort.

**Delightfully serves a party of 4**

2 cedar planks

4 – 10 oz. wild Alaskan salmon filets, skin on

Dave's All-Purpose Fish Seasoning

Maple Mayo Basting Sauce

1 sweet onion, thinly sliced

1 orange, sliced and rind removed

olive oil

Soak cedar planks in pure clean water overnight. Do not use tap water… buy bottled water!

Prepare your grill with charcoal and hickory or a fruitwood, like apple. If you can source pecan wood that's great, as pecan imparts a great smoky flavor to the salmon.

Prepare **Dave's All-Purpose Fish Seasoning** and **Maple Mayo Basting Sauce**.

Lightly season salmon filets with **Dave's All-Purpose Fish Seasoning**. Slather salmon filets with **Maple Mayo Basting Sauce**. Top filets with several thin slices of onion and place oranges, with rind removed, on top of onions.

Place cedar planks on grill grate for a few minutes to pre-season them with smoke. Open your grill, turn planks over, and quickly brush with olive oil. Place prepared salmon on the planks. Smoke for 12 to 15 minutes. Salmon should easily flake apart when finished. Remove salmon from the plank using a metal spatula, leaving the skin on the plank.

## DAVE'S ALL-PURPOSE FISH SEASONING

2 Tbsp. kosher salt

1 Tbsp. granulated garlic

1 Tbsp. lemon pepper

1 Tbsp. Aleppo chili pepper

2 tsp. chili powder

2 tsp. granulated onion powder

1 tsp. crushed dry basil

1 tsp. crushed dry oregano

1 tsp. fresh ground fennel seed
(do it yourself from seeds)

1/2 tsp. fresh ground black pepper

In a small bowl, mix ingredients together to create an amazing chicken or fish seasoning.

## MAPLE MAYO BASTING SAUCE

1/2 cup mayonnaise

3 Tbsp. pure thick maple syrup*

2 Tbsp. stone-ground mustard

*I highly recommend a good quality maple syrup which is thick and full of rich flavor. If you buy a cheaper maple syrup or pancake syrup, you need to reduce it to the thickness of honey.

If you have a thin maple syrup… take 1/2 cup of syrup and boil it down until it is thicker like honey and fuller tasting; cool before use.

Mix mayonnaise, maple syrup reduction, and mustard.

*Lightly season salmon filets with Dave's All-Purpose Fish Seasoning, then slather salmon filets with Maple Mayo Basting Sauce.*

Prepped
and ready
for the grill.

In the grill
smoking.

Finished!

PERSONALS

# WANTED
## IN ALASKA
# GOOD WOMAN

Able To Keep Me Warm At Night,
Cook, Sew And Clean House
**MUST BE ABLE TO CATCH FISH!**

**PLEASE SEND
PICTURE OF FISH!**

See how

*I love Alaska!! ready to move —
here's a picture of my fish!*

This page is dedicated to Tim Steinberg.
Tim is our Alaskan photographer friend who
sends us fresh salmon from Homer, AK!

175

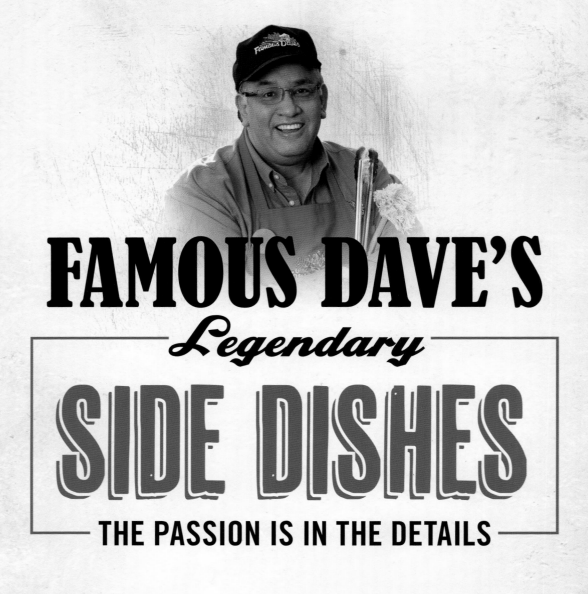

# FAMOUS DAVE'S
## *Legendary*
### SIDE DISHES
**THE PASSION IS IN THE DETAILS**

EAT ★ LAUGH ★ PARTY

# TABLE OF CONTENTS

# Fiesta Mexican Grilled Corn

**Your taste buds will be traveling south of the border for a fun Mexican fiesta!** It's a real mouthful of hollars when you taste these flavorful, fresh corncobs served up like Mexican street vendors. You can't eat just one… they're addicting. This recipe will make all other sweet corn recipes jealous!

---

### Delightfully serves a party of 4

**8 ears sweet corn, shucked**

**1/2 cup mayonnaise**

**1/4 cup vanilla yogurt**

**Chili Lime Pepper Shake**

**2 cup grated Cotija Añejo cheese**

**8 lime wedges**

Preheat an outdoor grill for medium-high heat. Grill corn until hot and lightly charred—up to 10 minutes.

Mix mayo with yogurt. Spread grilled corn evenly with yogurt mayonnaise mixture. Sprinkle lightly with **Chili Lime Pepper Shake**. Place crumbled cotija cheese on a plate and roll corn on the cheese.

Serve with a lime wedge.

*"Sex is good, but not as good as fresh, sweet corn!"*
~Garrison Keillor

# Chili Lime Pepper Shake

3 Tbsp. Famous Dave's Rib Rub
2 Tbsp. lime pepper
1 Tbsp. Aleppo chili powder

In a small bowl, mix the spices together.

YOU CAN DARN NEAR BET
WE'LL BE OPEN AT... 11:00
(LESSEN THE COOK DON'T SHOW)

ROUND ABOUT 10:00 AT NIGHT
THE CREW GETS THE ITCH TO
DO A LITTLE NIGHT FISHIN'
CATCH YA LATER!
★ FRI & SAT OPEN TILL 11:00 ★

HICKORY HEAVEN BAR-B-Q

ARMADILLO WILLY'S BARBECUE
GET SERIOUS ☆ GET WILLY'S

## Famous Dave's Hot Tips!

There are many different varieties of Mexican Cotija cheese. Some are very bland in flavor and are good for some recipes. For sweet corn, you want a fuller robust Cotija "Añejo" cheese. Añejo is the aged version like Parmesan... test a few varieties and find the one you like best! Attention to details, especially when it comes to flavor, is a serious priority when it comes to making the best party food!!!

# Mardi Gras "Almost" Dirty Rice

**This is no namby-pamby everyday rice dish! Down in the south... all southern cooks like to jack things up with over-the-top flavor and this rice dish is no exception.** You're going to love this festive rice salad that makes the perfect side dish to any party. It's almost a meal in itself.

---

## Delightfully serves a party of 6

1 lb. sausage, chopped, twice smoked & charred (like a smoked kielbasa)

2 large ears of fresh grilled sweet corn and sheared of niblets

1 lb. Jimmy Dean Regular Breakfast Pork Sausage, cooked & crumbled

1 cup onion, chopped

3 cups chicken broth

1-3/4 cups uncooked white rice

1 cup green bell pepper, diced

1 cup red bell pepper, diced

2 cloves fresh minced garlic

1 tsp. Louisiana Brand Hot Sauce

1/4 tsp. fresh ground black pepper

In a charcoal grill, twice smoke your store-bought smoked sausage using hickory or apple wood. After charring the sausage, slice into 1/2-inch slices.

While the grill is still hot, place sweet corn on the grill and cook until slightly charred.

In a large pan, cook the breakfast sausage while chopping it with your spatula to crumble. Once the sausage starts to brown, add onions. Once the onions start to turn translucent, add the rest of the ingredients. Bring to a boil. Cover and simmer for about 20 minutes. Make sure your rice is al dente... you don't want to be eating mush!

## BTW...

the reason I call this "almost" dirty rice is because a true Cajun dirty rice would be made with chicken livers and andouille sausage – I like my twice-smoked & charred sausage version better!

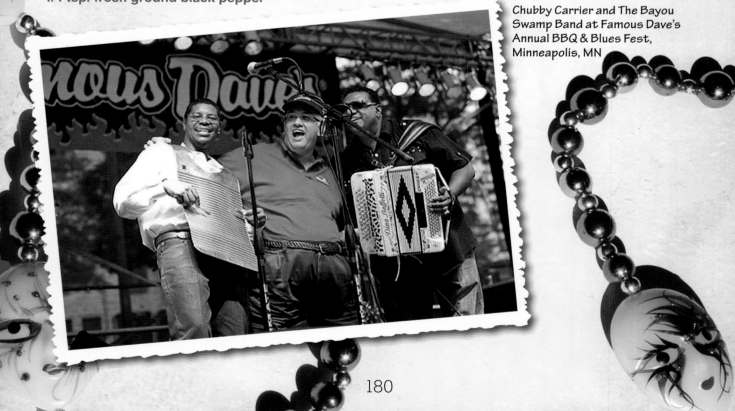

Chubby Carrier and The Bayou Swamp Band at Famous Dave's Annual BBQ & Blues Fest, Minneapolis, MN

# DAVE'S PARTY TIME BBQ BAKED BEANS

**These ain't your grannie's baked beans!** There are pumped-up flavors in this classic favorite: turbo-charged BBQ sauce with Kahlua, apricot preserves, jalapeños—seeds and all—twice-smoked sausage and then baked in the smoker for the flavor you love. If anyone ever said they hated beans… one taste of these and they'll be addicted forever!

## Delightfully serves a party of 10

**1 lb. Hillshire Farm Smoked Sausage Ring, smoked and charred**

**1 cup hickory-smoked bacon**

**1 cup Famous Dave's Rich & Sassy BBQ Sauce**

**1/2 cup apricot preserves**

**1 Tbsp. yellow prepared mustard**

**2 Tbsp. Kahlúa Liqueur**

**1 can** (28 oz.) **Bush's Baked Beans**

**1 can** (15 oz.) **Bush's Baked Beans**

**1 can** (14.5 oz.) **black beans**

**2 cans** (14.5 oz. size) **white beans**

**1 cup green bell pepper, diced**

**1/2 cup red bell pepper, diced**

**1 cup sweet onion, diced**

**1 jalapeño, NOT seeded, diced**

Get your grill smokin' and smoke the sausage over low smoke. In about an hour, your sausage will look good and smoky… char the sausage until the skin just starts to break. Remove and slice into 1/4-inch rounds, set aside.

Fry bacon until crispy. Chop and set aside.

Mix BBQ Sauce, apricot preserves, mustard, and Kahlua. Open all the bean cans. Drain the black and white beans. Leave the bean juice in the baked beans.

In a 9x13 pan that you are willing to put on a grill or smoker, place all the beans and add the BBQ sauce, peppers, onions, jalapeños, bacon, and the twice-smoked sausage. Place the pan in your grill or smoker and smoke at 300-degrees for 1 hour. If your grill is full, you can bake your beans in a 300-degree oven for 1 hour. I implore you to make every effort to bake your beans in a smoky grill because once you taste these amazing BBQ beans…your world will stop!

# Old Southern Honey Buttered Buttermilk Cornbread

**Folks who love their friends… feed them cornbread!** Nothing says "Good Old Southern Hospitality" like these made-from-scratch, honey buttered, cornbread muffins right out of the oven. These mouthwatering muffins are deliciously addicting and perfect for your next barbeque bash!

---

### Delightfully serves a party of 12

2/3 cup self-rising flour

2/3 cup Jiffy yellow cake mix*

1/3 cup yellow cornmeal

1/3 cup stone-ground yellow cornmeal

1/4 cup light brown sugar, packed

2 tsp. baking powder

1 tsp. salt

1 cup buttermilk

1/4 cup oil

1 egg, beaten

1/3 cup Hellman's Mayonnaise

*Optional add one large diced jalapeño or 8 ounces of fresh sweet corn*
*If you can't find Jiffy yellow cake mix… use the cheapest possible. The cheapest always seems to work best for cornbread!*

Preheat oven to 400 degrees. Prepare a muffin pan with muffin papers or spray muffin pans with non-stick cooking spray.

In a large bowl, mix flour, cake mix, yellow and stone-ground cornmeal, brown sugar, baking powder, and salt; set aside.

In a separate bowl, add buttermilk, oil, beaten egg, and mayonnaise, mix just enough to slightly blend ingredients. Pour wet ingredients into dry ingredients and lightly mix just until the dry ingredients are wet. Do not over mix.

Spoon into prepared muffin pan and bake for 25 minutes until tops are golden brown and the center are somewhat firm. A toothpick when inserted should be clean when removed. Hint: It's not necessary, but this batter works best when held overnight in a refrigerator… you'll get more rise on your muffin tops!

**If you have leftover cornbread see page 197 for Sweet Dixie's Cornbread Croutons recipe.**

## Honey Butter

1/4 cup clover honey

1/2 cup butter, softened

Whip butter with honey until well mixed. Immediately after removing cornbread from the oven, brush tops with Honey Butter… serve warm.

I like buying honey at my local Farmer's Market; the honey always seems so much richer in flavor.

"My definition of a balanced diet is...
a cornbread muffin in each hand!"
~Famous Dave Anderson

185

BETTER THAN MOM'S
CORN BREAD MUFFINS

# MISS MAMIE'S OLD SOUTHERN CORN FRITTERS

**One of the best things about summer is the first abundant harvest of sweet corn.** There isn't a better side dish for an old fashioned backyard get-together than a heaping pile of corn fritters. You can make them hush puppy style or like a pancake fritter. Dust them with powdered sugar, splash them with maple syrup, roll them in cinnamon sugar, or dunk them in homemade applesauce... it's all good!

**Delightfully serves a party of 4**

1/2 cup cornmeal

1/2 cup stone-ground cornmeal

1/2 cup flour

1/2 cup Jiffy Yellow Cake Mix

1 tsp. salt

1/4 tsp. cayenne pepper

2 tsp. baking powder

2 Tbsp. sugar

1 egg

1 cup whole milk

1 can (15 oz.) sweet corn, drained

2 Tbsp. melted butter

peanut oil for deep frying

In a large bowl, combine cornmeals, flour, cake mix, salt, cayenne, and baking powder in a mixing bowl.

In another bowl, whisk egg and sugar until sugar is dissolved. Add milk and combine. Add the milk mixture, sweet corn, and melted butter to the flour mixture and mix. Cover bowl with plastic wrap and let the batter rest in the refrigerator for 30 minutes.

Heat peanut oil in the deep fryer over medium heat to 375 degrees. Fry until they are a nice "darkish" golden brown... if they are too light it is almost certain that they will be doughy in the center.

**Yields:** 12 ping pong ball-size fritters.

**If you are making pancake type corn fritters...**
place enough oil to cover bottom of pan to a depth of about 1/4 inch and add 1/2 stick of butter. Use a large Teflon® spoon and spoon enough fritter dough into the oil to make a 3-inch pancake. Serve with a generous scoop of fresh **Homemade Applesauce** (pg. 199) and a dollop of sour cream.

**Yield:** 5 - 3-inch pancakes of about 4 ounces each.

# PEACHES & SWEET POTATO CASSEROLE

**Traditionally, sweet potato casseroles are a Thanksgiving dish, but this casserole is the perfect addition to any Bar-B-Que get-together any time of the year.** Folks are especially delighted to find peaches topping the sweet potatoes. And there ain't nothin' better than peaches, sweet potatoes, and pecans smothered in brown suga'! Peaches & Sweet Potato Casserole goes great with slow-smoked pork, smoked glazed hams, BBQ chicken, or brisket. Serve it warm or cold… it's all good! *PS: for a hint of old fashioned Southern flavor… add a shot of Jack Daniel's bourbon to the sweet potato mash!*

---

### Delightfully serves a party of 8

**5 large baked sweet potatoes**
(I prefer yams – they're sweeter!)

**1/3 cup dark brown sugar**

**2 eggs, beaten**

**1 tsp. salt**

**1 tsp. cinnamon**

**4 Tbsp. butter, melted**

**1/3 cup evaporated milk**

**1 tsp. vanilla extract**

**1 can** (16 oz.) **peach slices** (drained)
**or fresh in season**

### TOPPING

**2/3 cup all-purpose flour**

**3/4 cup light brown sugar**

**6 Tbsp. cold butter**

**1 cup pecans, rough chopped**

Preheat oven to 375 degrees. Place sweet potatoes on a cookie sheet and bake for 90 minutes. Let cool until they are cool enough to handle, and remove skins. Cut into cubes, then mash. Prepare a 9x13 casserole dish rubbed with butter.

In a large mixing bowl, combine sweet potatoes, brown sugar, eggs, salt, cinnamon, butter, milk, and vanilla extract. Using an electric mixer on low speed, mix until smooth. Place mixture in prepared casserole dish. Next, layer peaches on top of the sweet potato mash.

Prepare the topping: mix flour and brown sugar together. Cut in butter until mixture resembles coarse peas. Mix in pecans. Sprinkle topping evenly over the casserole. Bake at 350 degrees for 30-40 minutes until topping is bubbly and golden brown.

*** This recipe is the best because you bake the sweet potatoes instead of boiling them. Roasting the potatoes caramelizes the flavors rather than boiling the flavor out of the sweet potatoes.

## Famous Dave's Hot Tips!

1) Quickly skin baked potatoes by cutting the potatoes in half and squeezing the bottom end of the skin. The core of the potato slides right out!

2) Instead of mashing, use a potato ricer; the ricer reduces the stringiness of sweet potatoes.

3) Avoid last-minute frenzy! The casserole portion of this recipe and the topping can be made separately the day before and then refrigerated overnight. On the day of your party, bring casserole to room temperature and spread topping on top before baking.

*potato ricer*

# GRILLED VEGGIES

**My family loves grilled veggies and you're going to love these too!** While just throwing some vegetables on the grill is all it takes to create an excellent meal... marinating the veggies in a tasty robust citrus marinade will add some zippiness and interest to these everyday veggies. We especially love grilled veggies because you don't get that "squeakiness" like you do when you boil vegetables.

# Thrill of the grill...

**Delightfully serves a party of 6**

## VEGGIES

2 lbs. mini red or mini russet potatoes, quartered

1 lb. fresh asparagus

1 large red or sweet onion, halved, quartered, or sliced

1 lb. zucchini, halved lengthwise

1 red bell pepper, sliced

1 cup cherry tomatoes, sliced

splash of light olive oil

salt & pepper to taste

## VEGGIE MARINADE

1/2 cup light olive oil

1 cup white balsamic vinegar or rice wine vinegar

1/4 cup Famous Dave's Rich & Sassy BBQ Sauce

1/4 cup Asian sweet chili sauce

2 Tbsp. lemon juice

2 Tbsp. Dijon mustard

1 Tbsp. fresh garlic cloves, minced and crushed

1 tsp. salt

If you are smoking meats or have your smoker on... throw the potatoes into the smoker to get them tender before grilling. OR, if you're not smoking... I find it best to boil the potatoes for a few minutes before tossing them in the marinade. Do NOT marinate your potatoes if you smoke them; only marinate the potatoes if you boiled them to get them tender.

Prepare Veggie Marinade. In a bowl, combine all ingredients; mix well. Pour Veggie Marinade into a 2-gallon zip close plastic bag. Add washed veggies—except tomatoes. Marinate for 2 hours at room temperature.

Remove veggies and reserve marinade. Place veggies in a bowl and splash them with a little olive oil; season with kosher salt & pepper; toss to mix. Place veggies on your grill or if your grill has large grill grates and the veggies will fall through... use a grilling basket.

Place grilled veggies on a serving platter and add the cherry tomatoes... drizzle with reserved marinade (optional) and serve.

# Southwest Creamy Mac & Cheese

**This is not your Grandma's favorite mac & cheese recipe!** This is a spicy robust mac & cheese recipe that will make you forget mac & cheese ever came in a box. To get the full impact of the Southwest flavor… this mac is best served with a generous helping of the recommended toppings. This is a non-bake recipe which makes it the perfect choice for creating a "Mac & Cheese Bar" where your guests can dress their own mac with Southwest toppings that trip their trigger or float their boat. An interactive Mac & Cheese Bar with a good variety of toppings requires active participation which makes this recipe fun for parties!

*"Dude, macaroni and cheese is food of the Gods!"*
~Haley James Scott

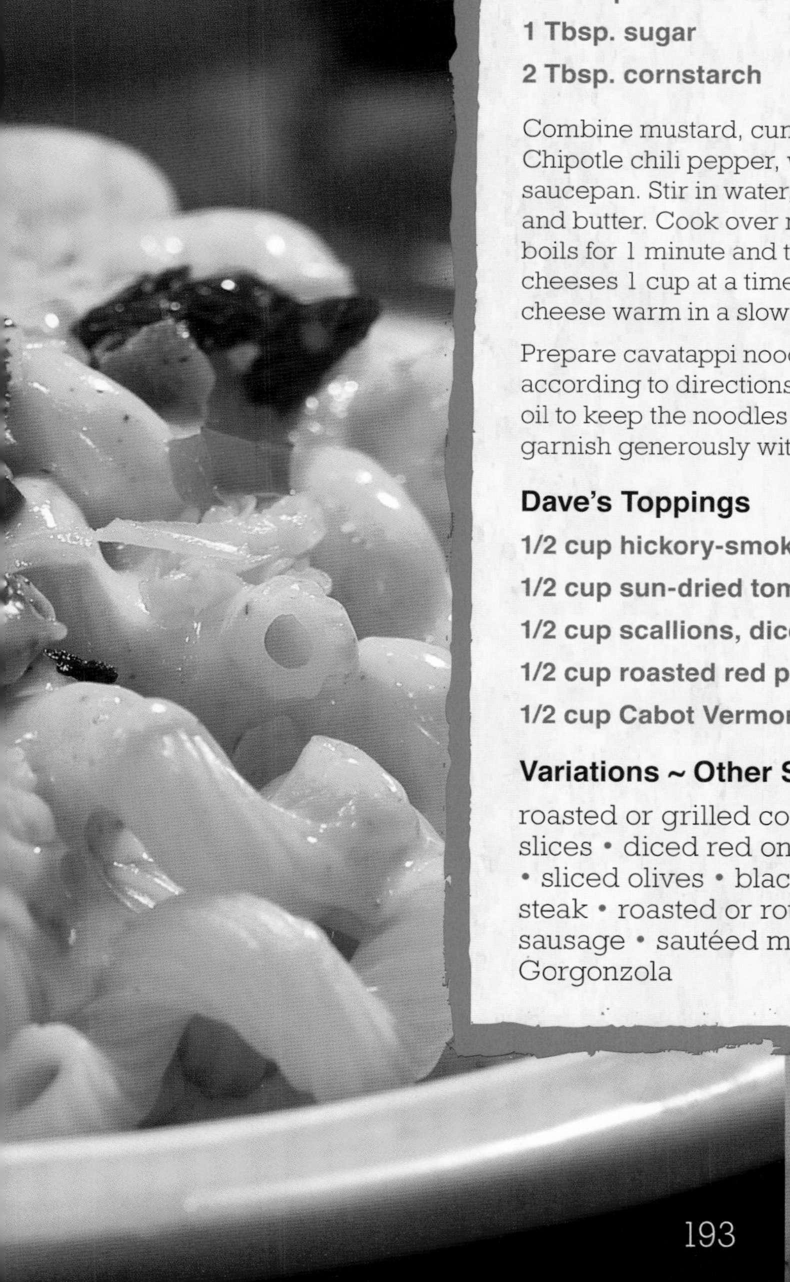

**Delightfully feeds a party of 6**

- **1 tsp. dry mustard**
- **2 tsp. cumin**
- **2 tsp. Aleppo chili pepper**
- **1 tsp. Ancho chili pepper**
- **1/2 tsp. Chipotle chili pepper in Adobe Sauce**
- **1/4 tsp. white pepper**
- **1-1/2 tsp. kosher salt**
- **1 Tbsp. sugar**
- **2 Tbsp. cornstarch**
- **1 cup water**
- **12 oz. Carnation Evaporated Milk**
- **1 cup half & half**
- **1/2 cup heavy cream**
- **3 Tbsp. salted butter**
- **8 oz. sharp Cheddar cheese, grated**
- **4 oz. Havarti cheese, grated**
- **3 oz. Parmesan cheese, grated**
- **1 box Italian cavatappi noodles**

Combine mustard, cumin, Aleppo chili pepper, Ancho chili pepper, Chipotle chili pepper, white pepper, salt, sugar, and cornstarch in a saucepan. Stir in water, evaporated milk, half & half, heavy cream, and butter. Cook over medium heat. Whisk until cream mixture boils for 1 minute and then immediately remove from heat. Add the cheeses 1 cup at a time and stir until cheese is fully melted. Keep cheese warm in a slow cooker until serving time.

Prepare cavatappi noodles or your choice of fun macaroni noodles according to directions. Once drained, splash lightly with light olive oil to keep the noodles from sticking. Serve with cheese sauce and garnish generously with toppings.

## Dave's Toppings

- **1/2 cup hickory-smoked bacon, chopped**
- **1/2 cup sun-dried tomatoes in olive oil**
- **1/2 cup scallions, diced**
- **1/2 cup roasted red pepper in olive oil, diced**
- **1/2 cup Cabot Vermont Extra Sharp Cheddar, grated**

## Variations ~ Other Southwest Topping Ingredients:

roasted or grilled corn • roasted red peppers • jalapeño slices • diced red onions • chopped cilantro • diced tomatoes • sliced olives • black beans • Parmesan cheese • grilled steak • roasted or rotisserie chicken • smoked & charred sausage • sautéed mushrooms • avocado • green onions • Gorgonzola

# HELL FIRE PICKLES & ONIONS

**FIRE UP All your grilled sandwiches, burgers, ribs, or veggies with these rip-roarin', flavor blasting Hell Fire Pickles & Onions!** For heaven's sakes, if you're going to go through all the trouble to throw a party…please, please, please…I beg you…don't go to the grocery store and grab plain old pickles, olives, mustards, and ketchup to put on your table. Just as important as making the best appetizers, the best burgers, and the best ribs… is topping off all your hard work with the best condiments that jump-start the soul of your taste buds. When you have the best pickles, a variety of great mustards, and even jacked-up ketchup… you create memorable meals that are over-the-top tasty.

---

## This makes 1 quart of Pure Awesomeness!

1 qt. fresh kosher dill pickles
(found in refrigerated section)

1 small sweet onion or red onion, sliced

1 cup sugar

1/3 cup coarse ground horseradish

3/4 cup white vinegar

1/4 cup water

2 tsp. pickling spice

1/4 tsp. celery seed

1 red jalapeño pepper, finely diced

Start with a great fresh-tasting pickle. Drain and reserve juice from pickles. Use a crinkle-cut knife and cut pickles into scalloped slices or just buy scalloped bread & butter pickles already sliced. Slice a sweet onion. Mix pickle slices with sliced onion. Place pickles and onions in a plastic container.

In a saucepan, mix sugar, horseradish, vinegar, water, pickling spice, celery seed, and red jalapeño; heat over low heat until sugar melts. Pour liquid over pickles and onions. Add reserved pickle juice if needed to cover pickles and onions. Put a lid on the plastic container and shake to mix. Refrigerate overnight before use.

SO MOUTH-TINGLING THESE PICKLES WILL MAKE YOU SHOUT… "O HELL YEAH!"

# SRIRACHA RED CABBAGE COLESLAW

**Oh my God... I have absolutely fallen in love with this stuff! ...both the coleslaw and the sauce by itself.** I could put this on everything. Use the coleslaw as an amazing side dish or a fantastic topping on all kinds of BBQ sandwiches. The sauce makes a great dipping sauce for all kinds of fruits or veggies. If your taste buds have been hibernating, this spicy hot chili coleslaw will knock your taste buds out of the deep freeze.

**Delightfully serves a party of 6**

1 head red cabbage, shredded

1/2 cup shredded carrot

2 cups mayonnaise

2 Tbsp. yellow mustard

2 Tbsp. fresh lemon juice

1/2 cup sugar

1/4 cup Sriracha hot chili sauce

1 Tbsp. fresh ground horseradish

1 tsp. kosher salt

1 cup fresh pineapple, diced (optional)

1/2 cup toasted almond slivers (optional)

Mix mayonnaise, yellow mustard, lemon juice, sugar, hot sauce, horseradish, and salt to make coleslaw dressing. Refrigerate one hour.

In a large bowl, shred cabbage and mix in carrots. Dress cabbage mixture with half of the coleslaw dressing. Refrigerate until ready to serve.

All coleslaw naturally weeps. Right before serving, drain the coleslaw and refresh it with the other half of the coleslaw dressing. Now add fresh pineapple and almond slivers (optional). Adding the almond slivers and pineapple at the end keeps them from turning purple like the cabbage.

# Sweet Dixie's Cornbread Croutons

Once you have a salad or a bowl of soup topped with your own homemade cornbread croutons… you're going to want them on everything! Cornbread croutons make everything come alive! I love homemade soups and growing up with a Southern dad, he was always putting cornbread in his chili. Today, I continue this tradition by making cornbread croutons for my soups. My family loves getting creative with salad toppings and creating our own variety of homemade salad dressings; however, we absolutely never ever spend good money on store-bought croutons. When I make cornbread muffins, I always make a second batch of batter just for croutons. For an added WOW, I like making my cornbread croutons more interesting by adding bacon, jalapeños, cheddar cheese, or sun-dried tomatoes. Your family and friends are going to love these homemade tasty treats in their salads or soups!

**Old Southern Honey Buttered Cornbread Muffin Ingredients (pg. 184)**

**melted butter**

Prepare the cornbread batter as directed in the **Old Southern Honey Buttered Cornbread Muffins** (pg. 184).

Pour batter into a non-stick sprayed 9x13 pan and bake croutons for 15 minutes. The larger 9x13 pan will give the cornbread a rise of less than an inch—perfect for croutons. After removing cornbread from oven… thoroughly cool.

Once cool, cut into crouton-size pieces. Preheat oven to 400 degrees. Place 1/2 of the pieces in a 9x13 pan and dab with melted butter. Toast for about 10 minutes. Repeat with the other half of the pieces. Let cool. Serve with salads or soups.

# Sassy Orange Sweet Potato Fries
## Featuring the Best-Tasting Dipping Sauce on the Planet!

These sassy orange sweet potato fries make a great side dish for any barbeque sandwich or entrée! What you'll discover is that the Sassy Orange Marshmallow Sauce is a real party for the mouth, but the combination of this tangy sauce and the sweet potato fries is just heavenly!

**Delightfully serves a party of 6**

2 lbs. sweet potatoes, peeled
and cut into french fries

peanut oil

kosher salt

Deep fry sweet potato fries in 375-degree oil to blanch them; this is about 3 to 4 minutes or when they start to have a crispness. Remove from oil and cool on a wire rack over a sheet pan or parchment placed on a sheet pan. Do not place fries on paper towels, it causes them to go limp.

Once cooled, return fries to 375 degree oil to finish frying them; approximately 3-4 minutes. Remove fries from oil and toss in a large metal bowl with kosher salt. Place on wire rack until ready to serve.

Serve with **Sassy Orange Marshmallow Sauce**.

## Sassy Orange Marshmallow Sauce

1 cup marshmallow cream

1/4 cup orange juice concentrate thawed

3/4 tsp. cinnamon

1/4 tsp. cayenne pepper

1/2 tsp. fine ground canning salt

1 Tbsp. fresh lemon juice

Mix marshmallow cream, orange juice concentrate, cinnamon, cayenne, canning salt, lemon juice and refrigerate until use.

*"I went into a McDonald's yesterday and said, 'I'd like some fries.' The girl at the counter said, 'Would you like some fries with that?'"*

~Jay Leno

# Homemade Applesauce

**This applesauce is amazingly delicious!** There's nothing better than homemade applesauce and it's healthy for you too. Making your own applesauce is easier than you think; once you've made your own homemade applesauce and tasted how fresh the flavors are... you'll never buy store-bought applesauce again.

---

**Delightfully serves a party of 6**

3 Red Delicious apples

3 Granny Smith apples

2 Gala apples

2 Fuji apples

2 Honey Crisp apples

2 cups purified water

2 tsp. cinnamon

1/8 tsp. nutmeg

A great applesauce needs a variety of apples to give it a well-rounded flavor. You do not have to use the apples listed... use whatever is in season, mixing equal numbers of sweet and tart apples. If you prefer a sweet applesauce, use a higher ratio of sweet apples.

Use an apple corer to skin, core, and slice apples. Remove any inside seed shells from the apples. Place water in the bottom of a heavy stock pot and bring to boil. Add apples and lemon juice; bring back to a boil. Turn heat to low; add cinnamon and nutmeg. Simmer apples until they are soft. Remove from heat and lightly mash with potato masher if you like a chunky applesauce. If you prefer a smoother applesauce, run through a ricer. Let cool.

# Best Cranberry Sauce Ever!

**The secret to this sauce is no sugar... just tasty fruit juice concentrate.** Once you taste this beautiful cranberry sauce you will agree that it shouldn't just be for Thanksgiving. This delightful, somewhat semi-tart cranberry sauce makes a wonderful accompaniment for anything any time of the year.

**Delightfully serves a party of 8**

**1 large seedless navel orange pureed in food processor** (yes, the whole thing!)

**1 lb fresh cranberries**

**1 cup orange juice concentrate**

**1 cup apple juice concentrate**

**1 large apple, skinned and grated**

**1/2 cup dried cherries**

**1/2 cup dried cranberries**

**1/2 cup golden raisins**

**1 cup pecans, chopped** (optional)

**1/2 tsp. salt**

**1/4 tsp. cinnamon**

Wash and clean the orange. Slice the orange into eighths, removing both ends and lightly puree the orange in a food processor.

In a large saucepan, place cranberries, pureed orange, and remaining ingredients. Cover and let simmer. Stir occasionally. Continue simmering until cranberries fully burst—about 15 minutes.

Remove from heat, cool down, and refrigerate overnight. Refrigerate your serving dish before filling. Serve cold.

## Famous Dave's Hot Tips!

Be adventurous and top off a grilled chicken breast sandwich with this sauce or fling a dollop of it over a veggie omelet.

*"All over America at Thanksgiving time, can openers are opening up tin cans filled with cranberry jelly... it's about the same as if plastic cartons filled with processed turkey slices were placed on the table. YUK! Fresh cranberry sauce is incredibly easy to make... so enjoy these wonderful gifts of nature."*

~Famous Dave Anderson

# GRILLED CORN & HERB BUTTERS

**One of the joys of summer is fresh-picked sweet corn.** Grilling corn is all about caramelizing the sugars in corn over an open fire. I have to admit I am an uncontrollable live fire addict… if it were up to me, I'd throw everything on the grill! If I am just grilling corn for my family, it's easy to wrap each corn in foil with butter and precook before grilling them. Forget about trying to cook corn in husks—it's too bothersome and messy. When I cook for a large party, it's much easier to parboil the corn and then throw them on the grill right before serving time. What I like so much about grilled corn is that fresh-picked corn is smacked full of natural sugars and grilling brings out their natural goodness. Then, when you slather this corn with these robust kicked-up butters… you're in for a real treat. These recipes are only a starting point to get you experimenting… have fun figuring out your own secret spiked butter concoctions for your next party!

**Delightfully serves a party of 6**

**12 ears of fresh-picked sweet corn**

Prepare corn by husking and removing all corn silk. Boil corn in salt water for 8-10 minutes. Finish on the grill to caramelize the natural corn sugars. Brush with melted butter. Serve with Herb Butters.

## Fresh Strawberries & Sun-dried Tomato Butter

2 cups butter, softened

1/2 cup sun-dried tomatoes in oil, drained and finely diced

2 cups strawberries with core removed, finely diced

1 tsp. coarse ground sea salt

1/2 tsp. coarse ground black pepper

1 tsp. Aleppo chili pepper

Prepare the ingredients for the butter; once butter is softened, thoroughly mix the ingredients into butter. Place into a plastic-covered container. Place the container in the fridge until needed. On the day of your party, remove the herb butter from the fridge 1 hour before serving, to soften.

## Wasabi Lime Herb Butter

2 cups butter, softened

4 Tbsp. fresh basil, finely minced, packed

2 Tbsp. fresh chives, finely minced

1/4 cup fresh lime juice

2 tsp. grated lime zest

2 Tbsp. Inglehoffer Wasabi Horseradish

1 tsp. coarse ground sea salt

1/2 tsp. coarse ground black pepper

Prepare the ingredients for the butter; once butter is softened, thoroughly mix the ingredients into butter. Place into a plastic-covered container. Place the container in the fridge until needed. On the day of your party, remove the herb butter from the fridge 1 hour before serving, to soften.

## Dijon Horseradish Butter

2 cups butter, softened

4 Tbsp. Dijon mustard

4 Tbsp. fresh ground horseradish

2 tsp. granulated garlic

1 tsp. coarse ground sea salt

1/2 tsp. coarse ground black pepper

1/4 tsp. cayenne pepper

Prepare the ingredients for the butter; once butter is softened, thoroughly mix the ingredients into butter. Place into a plastic-covered container. Place the container in the fridge until needed. On the day of your party, remove the herb butter from the fridge 1 hour before serving, to soften.

## Famous Dave's Hot Tips!

I always make the butters several days before so the flavors fully blossom. Then I soften the butters a bit before serving so they are easy to spoon into serving dishes.

These are only a few of my herb butter recipes. I encourage you, once you've made these recipes… start figuring out your own tasty butters for the next time you grill. And one more thing, these butters are excellent on toasty breads or as toppings for grilled steaks. Enjoy!

# VEGGIE KABOBS
## with Sun-dried Tomato Balsamic Vinaigrette

**Take your party to the next level with these festive veggie kabobs.** Sure I have a grilled tossed veggie recipe in this cookbook, which is great for large parties… but if you want to really dress up your serving table, these kabobs are the bomb!

**Delightfully serves a party of 8**

4 large portobello mushrooms

2 red onions

3 zucchinis

2 yellow squash

1 green bell pepper

1 yellow bell pepper

1 red bell pepper

1 pint cherry tomatoes

kosher salt

fresh ground black pepper

wooden or metal kabob skewers

Prepare **Sun-dried Tomato Balsamic Vinaigrette**. Prep all veggies except tomatoes by slicing them into large enough pieces for skewering. All the veggies should be approximately the same size to grill evenly. Place veggies in a large 2-gallon sealable plastic bag. Pour the **Sun-dried Tomato Balsamic Vinaigrette** over veggies and refrigerate for 2 hours.

After two hours, remove veggies from bag and save marinade. Skewer veggies and place on a medium heat grill. Baste veggies with reserved marinade.

Garnish skewers with carved cherry tomatoes after grilling (placing the cherry tomatoes on the skewers after grilling keeps them from falling into your grill!).

# Sun-dried Tomato Balsamic Vinaigrette

1/2 cup sun-dried tomatoes in oil

3/4 cup white balsamic vinegar

1 Tbsp. fresh lemon juice

3 fresh garlic cloves, minced and smashed

2 Tbsp. fresh basil leaves, minced

2 tsp. fresh oregano leaves, minced

1 tsp. canning salt

1/4 tsp. fresh ground black pepper

1 cup extra virgin olive oil

Place sun-dried tomatoes, balsamic vinegar, lemon juice, garlic, basil, oregano, salt, and pepper in a blender and blend until smooth. Slowly drizzle olive oil into the blender until the mixture is emulsified.

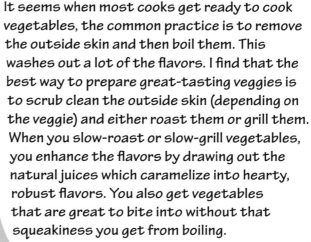

It seems when most cooks get ready to cook vegetables, the common practice is to remove the outside skin and then boil them. This washes out a lot of the flavors. I find that the best way to prepare great-tasting veggies is to scrub clean the outside skin (depending on the veggie) and either roast them or grill them. When you slow-roast or slow-grill vegetables, you enhance the flavors by drawing out the natural juices which caramelize into hearty, robust flavors. You also get vegetables that are great to bite into without that squeakiness you get from boiling.

# FRUIT KABOBS

**Add energy to your Party table with these fun and colorful fruit kabobs.** I like kabobs because they can serve a large number of people fast. All your party guests have to do is pick up a skewer and they are off to the next offering instead of holding up the line while they contemplate what to eat. The fruit dip is to die for; you'll watch people come back just to grab more fruit dip!

*Avoid fruits and nuts... You are what you eat!* ~Jim Davis

**Delightfully Serves a party of 12**

1 quart strawberries

1 pineapple

6 kiwis

4 oranges

1 bunch red or green seedless grapes

2 star fruits

12 skewers

You can really use any fruit that you like. Apples and bananas are not the best choices as they will turn color. Prepare fruit into appropriate sizes for skewering, about 2 inches in length and height. I like using interesting fruits like kiwis or star fruits and finishing with a grape on top of the skewer to dress it up.

# FRUIT DIP

7 oz. marshmallow creme

8 oz. strawberry flavored cream cheese, room temperature*

8 oz. heavy whipping cream

3 Tbsp. powdered sugar

1/4 cup orange juice concentrate

1 tsp. vanilla extract

1/4 cup fresh strawberries, lightly pureed

*If you can't find strawberry cream cheese that's OK… plain cream cheese will do just fine.

Beat cream cheese with an electric mixer to fluff it up, then add marshmallow creme. Mix cream cheese and marshmallow creme well and set aside.

Place one pint of heavy whipping cream into a $CO_2$ type whipped cream dispenser along with 3 heaping tablespoons of powder sugar and 1 teaspoon vanilla extract. Place the whipped cream dispenser in the refrigerator for two hours.

After two hours, using the whipped cream dispenser, release 1/2 of the fresh whipped cream or about 3 cups of whipped cream into the marshmallow mixture and add the orange juice concentrate.

Gently fold in strawberries and mix with a wire whip until all ingredients are combined; don't over stir. This is important… refrigerate dip for at least two hours before use.

## Famous Dave's Hot Tips!

To make getting the marshmallow creme out of the jar easier, run hot water over your spatula.

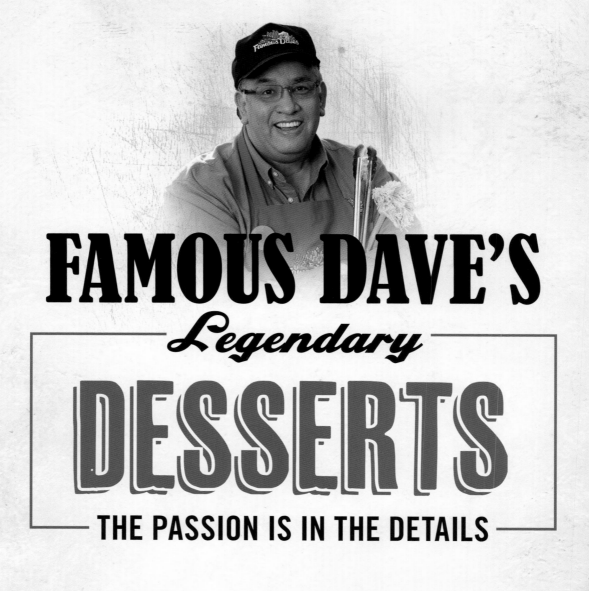

# FAMOUS DAVE'S

## *Legendary*

# DESSERTS

## THE PASSION IS IN THE DETAILS

# EAT ★ LAUGH ★ PARTY

# TABLE OF CONTENTS

# Old Fashioned Banana Pudding

**This banana pudding is a real Southern treat!** My dad is from the south and I know my banana puddings… I guarantee this will be the best banana pudding you've ever tasted! I like this recipe because it's quick and easy—unlike the baked version. Plus, the rich whipped cream that is folded into the pudding makes this recipe nothing but pure pleasure. A great banana pudding goes with any menu… it's old-fashioned, soul-soothing, comfort on a spoon! I believe this is what the angels eat in heaven!

## Delightfully serves a party of 8

**6 fresh bananas, sliced**

**8 oz. cream cheese, room temperature**

**7 oz. sweetened condensed milk**

**1 - small package instant vanilla pudding mix**

**1/2- small package** (3.9 oz.) **of instant banana cream pudding mix**

**2-1/2 cups cold whole milk**

**1/4 tsp. salt**

**1 tsp. vanilla extract**

**2 pints fresh whipping cream, 1 pint for pudding and 1 pint for topping** (Whipped Cream Dispenser see Grilling Tips pg. 31)

**1 Tbsp. powdered sugar**

**1 tsp. pure vanilla extract**

**Ball Fruit-Fresh Produce Protector**

**Pepperidge Farm Butter Chessman Cookies**

**fresh mint sprigs** (optional)

## Famous Dave's Hot Tips!

I love Ball's Fruit-Fresh Protector. Usually you are instructed to use diluted lemon juice to keep things like apples, bananas, pears, and avocados from turning brown… but they almost always pick up some sourness from the lemon. Ball Fruit-Fresh Produce Protector is a little bit sweet and works like a charm. I love this stuff!

In a large bowl, fluff room temperature cream cheese with a mixer. Add condensed milk and continue mixing. Make sure your cream cheese and condensed milk mixture is well creamed. This helps to add air, which adds thickness to the pudding.

In a separate bowl, mix the vanilla pudding and banana pudding. Add cold milk, salt, and vanilla extract; mix well. Add to the cream cheese mixture and blend together. Place pudding in refrigerator for at least two hours—or make the day before.

Place one pint of heavy whipping cream into a CO2 type Whipped Cream Dispenser along with 1 heaping tablespoon of powder sugar and 1 teaspoon vanilla extract. Place the whipped cream dispenser in the refrigerator for two hours.

After two hours, give the pudding mixture a couple of quick strokes using a wire whip to loosen it up. In a separate bowl, whip the second pint of whipping cream with a mixer until soft peaks form. Fold whipped cream into pudding mixture.

Slice bananas and put into Ball's Fruit-Fresh Protector. Spoon a couple tablespoons of pudding mixture into the bottom of a small glass jar. Top this with sliced bananas, then another layer of the pudding mixture. Repeat layer. Refrigerate until your party starts.

Right before serving, dispense a topping of whipping cream on top of the pudding and garnish with Chessman cookies, banana slices, and a mint sprig.

**Variation:** You can also layer the pudding in a 9x13 glass casserole dish if you don't have the time to individualize the servings. However, if you are going to use a 9x13 casserole dish, then I would go back to using the traditional vanilla wafers for layering.

# RASPBERRY CHEESECAKE MINIS

**Oreo Cookies, Raspberries, and Creamy Cheesecake...** these Mini Raspberry Cheesecake muffins are the perfect little dessert for any party—or just to make your family happy! They're delightfully colorful and absolutely delicious. Just a word of caution, if you pop these tasty little treats into your own mouth before your guests arrive... you won't be able to stop. Before you know it... SURPRISE!!! you have nothing for your party. Go ahead and make a double batch—you're going to want a few extras!

**Delightfully serves a party of 6**

## OREO CRUST

6 Tbsp. butter, room temperature

1/3 cup sugar

3 cups Oreo cookies, cream center removed

## CREAM CHEESE FILLING

16 oz. Philadelphia Cream Cheese, softened at room temperature

1/2 cup sugar

2 eggs

1/2 cup sour cream

1 tsp. vanilla

1 Tbsp. all-purpose flour

## RASPBERRY GLAZE FILLING

10 oz. frozen raspberries, thawed

1/4 cup pure filtered water

1 Tbsp. cornstarch

1/4 cup sugar

## GARNISH

1 pint fresh raspberries

powder sugar

*You can get greaseproof muffin liners online.

## OREO CRUST

Prepare a mini muffin tray with greaseproof paper baking cups* and spray muffin cups with a nonstick cooking spray. Combine butter and sugar. Place cookies in food processor and pulse until finely pulverized. Don't turn cookies into dust! Mix cookie crumbs with butter mixture. Press cookie mixture into the bottom of each muffin cup. I like to use the cap from a Famous Dave's BBQ sauce bottle to tap the cookie mixture solidly into the bottom of the muffin cup. Place in refrigerator until ready to use.

## CREAM CHEESE FILLING

Preheat oven to 375 degrees. Using an electric mixer, beat cream cheese and sugar until combined. Add eggs one at a time and beat until the mixture is combined; careful not to over beat. Next, mix in sour cream, vanilla, and flour until smooth. Spoon filling into muffin cups to 3/4 full. Bake about 15 minutes or until filling is set. Place on wire rack and cool at room temperature. Refrigerate at least 4 hours or overnight. Your mini cheesecake muffins may cave in the middle, which is OK because you can fill this in with the raspberry glaze filling.

## RASPBERRY GLAZE FILLING

In a bowl, smash thawed raspberries and strain. Discard raspberry mash and reserve the juice. Take reserved raspberry juice and add enough water to measure 1 cup of liquid (approx. 1/4 cup) and place in a saucepan. In a small bowl, mix cornstarch and sugar; add mix to raspberry juice. Heat to boil. Reduce heat and boil for one minute while stirring. Cool until mixture starts to thicken like jelly, but is still spoon-able. Spoon on top of cheesecakes.

Garnish each cheesecake mini with three fresh raspberries. Return minis to the refrigerator. Sprinkle with powder sugar before serving.

**Yields:** 12 mini cheesecakes.

*"Health food may be good for the conscience but Oreos taste ... a hell of a lot better!"*
*~Robert Redford*

# Country Fresh Peach Cobbler

**The ultimate indulgence...fresh from-the-oven peach cobbler is one of America's most favorite desserts!** Celebrate all the fun of summer with this moist flavorful cobbler that is a snap to make... and so tasty it will even have Grandma begging for the recipe! A very delicious dessert served warm with a dollop of fresh whipped cream or homemade vanilla ice cream.

This is a very versatile recipe... try adding other tasty fruits like raspberries, strawberries, blueberries, or even rhubarb... ENJOY!

**Delightfully serves a party of 8**

## FILLING

8 cups peeled, sliced fresh peaches

3/4 cup sugar

2 Tbsp. powdered Country Time Lemonade

2 tsp. cinnamon

1/4 tsp. nutmeg

1/2 tsp. salt

1/2 cup water

8 Tbsp. butter

## BATTER MIX

1-1/2 cups self-rising flour

1 cup sugar

1/4 tsp. salt

1 cup whole milk

1/2 cup buttermilk

1/2 tsp. vanilla extract

## TOPPING

1 egg, beaten

3 Tbsp. half & half

1 Tbsp. sugar

1 Tbsp. raw sugar or turbinado raw sugar

### FILLING

Preheat oven to 350 degrees. Combine fresh sliced peaches, 3/4 cup sugar, lemonade, cinnamon, nutmeg, salt, and water in a saucepan and mix well. Bring to a boil and simmer for 10 minutes. Remove from the heat. Put the butter in a 3-quart baking dish and place in oven to melt.

### BATTER MIX

Mix 1 cup sugar, salt, flour, buttermilk, and vanilla—slowly to prevent clumping. Whisk just until somewhat smooth. Do not over mix as the batter will turn stretchy! Gently pour mixture over melted butter. Do not stir. Gently spoon filling mixture on top. Do not stir. Batter will rise to top during baking. Bake for 30 minutes.

### TOPPING

To make egg wash, mix one egg with half & half and set aside. In another bowl, mix the sugar with the raw sugar.

After 30 minutes, remove cobbler from oven and brush small areas with egg & cream mixture. Quickly sprinkle sugars over cobbler where you have applied egg wash; repeat until entire cobbler is sugared. For best results, do not try and brush entire surface with egg wash as it will dry before you can add your sugars. Place back in oven for another 15 minutes until batter has set and sugars on top have caramelized.

To serve, scoop onto a plate and serve with your choice of fresh whipped cream or dairy fresh, natural vanilla bean, old-fashioned custard-type ice cream.

**FOR CANNED PEACHES:** While I recommend fresh...you can use canned peaches. You will need 8 cups of peaches including some juice for fill. Discard extra juice. Combine with Country Time Lemonade, cinnamon, nutmeg, and salt. You will NOT need to add sugar or water when using canned peaches.

# Jus'Pic'd Fresh Strawberry Chocolate Cupcakes

## *A Strawberry Lover's Delight!*

**Nothing says "Hello, Summer" like farm fresh "Jus'Pic'd," juicy, sweet strawberries.** Anyone who's ever picked fresh, vine-ripened strawberries right out of a strawberry patch knows there's no comparison to what's sold in grocery stores. If you're out in the country and you see a roadside farmer selling fresh strawberries… don't even think twice—stop and pick some up! These Strawberry Chocolate Cupcakes are floated on a puddle of strawberry daiquiri mix, smothered in a deep chocolate ganache, topped with strawberry cream cheese, and crowned with a beautiful, mouthwatering, chocolate-dipped strawberry. This delightful summer dessert is easy to make and will absolutely WOW your guests.

**Delightfully makes 24 cupcakes**

1 box Pillsbury Moist Supreme Classic White cake mix

3 Tbsp. all-purpose flour

1 cup pureed fresh strawberries

1/2 cup strawberry daiquiri mix

3/4 cup vegetable oil

4 eggs

3 cups strawberry daiquiri mix for plating

Chocolate Ganache

Strawberry Cream Cheese Frosting

Chocolate-Dipped Strawberries

Set oven to 350 degrees. Prepare cupcake pans with cupcake liners; lightly spray liners with non-stick cooking spray.

In a mixing bowl, combine cake mix and flour; set aside. In a blender, add enough fresh strawberries to make one cup when pureed. Add strawberry daiquiri mix to the strawberry puree. Pour strawberry mixture into cake mixture.

In a small bowl, beat eggs and add to cake mixture. Add oil and beat for 2 minutes. Pour batter into cupcake liners filling only halfway. Cupcakes should rise to the top of the baking cups. These cupcakes need to be flat on top so they don't roll over when you frost them upside down.

Bake 15 minutes to 20 minutes; until inserted toothpick comes out clean. Cool on a wire rack for 10 minutes, then remove cupcakes from liners and turn upside down to finish cooling. Cupcakes need to be completely cooled before frosting.

While the cupcakes are cooling, prepare the **Strawberry Cream Cheese Frosting** (pg. 218) and **Chocolate Ganache** (pg. 218).

Line a metal sheet pan with wax paper. Once cooled, place upside-down cupcakes—one by one— on one corner of a wire rack. Hold the wire rack over the ganache saucepan and spoon ganache over the cupcake. Allow the extra ganache to fall back into the saucepan. If the ganache starts to become stiff, warm the saucepan to gently soften.

Set the wire rack down. Use a pie server and fork to gently slide the cupcake onto the wax paper. Let cupcake sit for 20 minutes to allow the ganache to "set" before moving it onto the serving dish.

Prepare serving plates by placing two tablespoons of strawberry daiquiri mix on the center of each plate.

Once the ganache has set, use the pie slicer/server to pick up the cupcake and place it in the middle of the daiquiri-juiced plate. The cupcake will "wick" the strawberry daiquiri mix and make the insides of the cupcake even more flavorsome and moist.

Place a dollop of **Strawberry Cream Cheese Frosting** (pg. 218) on top. Finish with a **Chocolate-Dipped Strawberry** on top. Garnish plate with strawberry slices.

## Famous Dave's Hot Tips!

This recipe calls for strawberry daiquiri mix to be floated on the plate, but if you want to add a shot of rum to the mix and then place the cupcakes on top of this... it will certainly rock your cupcakes!

# CHOCOLATE-DIPPED STRAWBERRIES

**2 lbs. strawberries**
**Chocolate Ganache**

Wash strawberries and dry thoroughly on a paper towel. Dry strawberries are vital to dipping, but do not wash until you are ready to use. Next, separate the big strawberries from the small strawberries. You will want to use the big strawberries for pureeing and the small ones for dipping and garnishing.

Take a metal sheet pan and place it in the freezer for 1/2 hour. Prepare **Chocolate Ganache**. Remove pan from the freezer and place freezer paper on the bottom of the pan with the shiny side up. Dip your strawberries in ganache and place on the freezer paper. The cold metal pan will help your strawberries set the chocolate faster.

Even though my **Chocolate Ganache** recipe is created for cupcakes, it is soft enough to use with the strawberries, too. Usually you wouldn't use butter in a chocolate dip for strawberries… but here it's OK since the strawberries will be sitting on top of a cream cheese frosting.

**Note:** you won't need 2 lbs of strawberries, but it's better to have a quantity to find the best-looking berries for dipping and garnishing. What you don't use… dip in leftover ganache and indulge yourself!

# CHOCOLATE GANACHE

**10 oz. bittersweet chocolate, finely chopped**
**1 cup heavy whipping cream**
**3 Tbsp. butter, softened to room temperature**

Finely chop chocolate using a serrated knife. Place chopped chocolate in a medium sauce pan and set aside.

In a small sauce pan, bring heavy whipping cream almost to a boil and then immediately turn off the heat. Pour hot whipping cream over the chopped chocolate. Let it sit for a few minutes until the chocolate looks melted. Using a whisk, gently stir until smooth. Add softened butter and whisk until ganache is smooth and glistens. Leave saucepan on warm stove top until needed.

# STRAWBERRY CREAM CHEESE FROSTING

**8 oz. Philadelphia Cream Cheese, softened**
**1 stick butter, softened**
**2 cups powdered sugar**
**3 Tbsp. strawberry daiquiri mix**

Place cream cheese in mixing bowl with softened butter. Mix until blended. Add powdered sugar, 1/4 cup at a time, mixing thoroughly. Mix in strawberry daiquiri mix. Place bowl in refrigerator until needed.

## Famous Dave's Hot Tips!

When you're prepping strawberries for a party, it's tedious to core a lot strawberries. These hullers make coring strawberries a snap.

It's been said, "You are known by the company you keep!"

# Black Iron Skillet Apple Crisp

**This is the apple crisp recipe your grandma wished she could get her hands on… guaranteed!** Today, people's time is so precious that when they actually take time to cook in their own kitchen they don't want to make just any recipe… they want to cook the best recipe in the world! Well this is "The World's Best Apple Crisp Ever." I have to give credit to my daughter-in-law Colleen for this crazy-good apple crisp recipe. I like to make apple crisp in a cast iron skillet because it adds a certain "old fashioned warmth" to my baking. There is something "soul comforting" about placing a cast iron skillet brimming with bubbly apple crisp on the family table along with homemade ice cream!

**Delightfully serves a party of 6**

## TOPPING

1 cup flour

2/3 cup brown sugar, packed

1/3 cup white sugar

1 cup old fashioned oatmeal

1 tsp. cinnamon

1 tsp. salt

1 stick + 3 Tbsp. unsalted butter

## FILLING

1/2 cup apple juice concentrate

1 Tbsp. fresh lemon juice

2 lbs. Jonathan apples*

1 lb. Gala apples*

1/3 cup granulated white sugar

1-1/2 tsp. cinnamon

2 Tbsp. unsalted butter

(*see Famous Dave's Helpful Tips below)

## FILLING

In a cup, mix lemon juice with apple juice concentrate and set aside.

Prepare apples by peeling, coring, and cutting them into 1/2-inch slices and place in a large bowl. Mix sugar and cinnamon together and sprinkle over apple slices; toss to evenly coat slices and set filling aside.

## TOPPING

Prepare the topping. In a medium-size bowl, combine flour, brown sugar, granulated sugar, oats, cinnamon, and salt. Cut in butter until topping is crumbly about the size of big peas. Break up any large clumps and set topping aside.

Prepare oven by placing rack in the middle position. Preheat to 450 degrees. Heat a large cast iron skillet over medium heat and melt 2 tablespoons of butter. Once the butter is melted, add the cinnamon apple mixture to skillet. Stir frequently; cook until the apples begin to turn translucent around the edges. You only want to soften the apples; be careful to not overcook and turn the apples into mush.

Remove skillet from heat and pour lemon apple juice concentrate into skillet; fold in apples to combine well. Spread topping evenly over apples. Place the skillet on a sheet pan and place in oven. Bake 17 to 20 minutes until the filling is bubbling and the topping is a deep golden brown. Remove from oven and set on a wire rack. Serve warm with ice cream and fresh whipping cream.

### Directions for a 9x13 baking dish

If you do not have an iron skillet… use a 9x13-inch baking dish. Set your oven to 350 degrees. Combine filling ingredients and place in baking dish. Prepare topping as directed above and spread over apples. Place baking dish on a sheet pan and bake for one hour until filling is bubbling and topping is a deep golden brown.

## Famous Dave's Hot Tips!

The key to making great apple crisp is doing your homework. Every month certain apples are tastier than others, depending on when they were harvested. When I make apple crisp, I buy every available apple at that time of year. Knowing what flavor, sweetness, and tartness is available for your apple crisp is one of the keys to making a great-tasting apple crisp.

221

# Old Fashioned Carrot Cake

Whether you're enjoying a warm sunny day or watching big fluffy snowflakes fall from the sky... there isn't anything more soothing to the soul than fond memories of a home filled with the delightful aromas of a just-baked, old fashioned carrot cake that Mom was taking out of the oven! This is one of my most requested dessert recipes as folks just can't get over how moist and flavorful this cake tastes. I'll guarantee you that you'll never taste a better carrot cake that is so delicious and mouthwateringly tasty!

**Delightfully serves a party of 1**
(if you must share, this cake will serve 2. Oh alright... if you really have to spread the happiness around... you can get 12 big slices if you don't eat it all yourself first!)

**2-1/2 cups all-purpose flour**

**2 tsp. baking soda**

**1-1/2 tsp. baking powder**

**1-1/2 tsp. salt**

**1-1/2 tsp. cinnamon**

**3 eggs**

**1 cup canola oil**

**3/4 cup buttermilk**

**1-1/2 cups sugar**

**2 tsp. vanilla extract**

**1 can** (8oz.) **crushed pineapple, lightly drained**

**2 cups carrot, finely grated**

**1 cup sweetened coconut flakes**

**1 cup baking raisins**

**1 1/2 cups walnuts, chopped**

**cream cheese frosting**

In a small bowl, sift flour, baking soda, baking powder. salt, and cinnamon. Set aside.

In a large mixing bowl, beat eggs. Add oil, buttermilk, sugar, and vanilla; mix well. Add into the dry ingredients, blending thoroughly. Mix in the pineapple, carrots, coconut, raisins, and 1 cup walnuts.

Pour into a greased and floured 9x13 baking pan. Bake in a 350-degree oven for 50 minutes or until a toothpick inserted in the center comes out clean.

Cool completely before frosting… or the cream cheese frosting will melt on you! Garnish with remaining walnuts.

## CREAM CHEESE FROSTING

6 Tbsp. butter, softened

8 oz. cream cheese, softened

3 to 4 cups powdered sugar (to desired sweetness)

1 tsp. vanilla

2 Tbsp. heavy cream

In a medium bowl, blend butter and cream cheese. Slowly add powdered sugar one cup at a time. Blend in vanilla and heavy cream until creamy smooth. Frost completely cooled cake. Serve immediately or refrigerate cake, as frosting contains fresh dairy products.

Escape everyday boring...
this Pineapple Cove Rum Cake
is an island vacation on a plate!

# Pineapple Cove Rum Cake

**There's a reason why Pirates hung around the islands... fresh pineapples, rum, plunder, and beach parties!** This delicious pineapple dessert is worthy of any pirate party. You'll never fear walking the plank when you serve this treasure of a dessert. Grilled fresh pineapple, buttery grilled pound cake, and peaches drizzled with **Caramel Rum Sauce**. ARRGH!

---

### Delightfully serves a Swashbuckling Pirate Party of 6

2 fresh pineapples

6 fresh peaches or quick-frozen peaches

1 loaf pound cake

1/2 cup unsalted butter, melted

1 cup Captain Morgan Spiced Rum

Caramel Rum Sauce

strawberries (garnish)

Start grill. Remove skin from pineapples and slice into 2" planks. Grill pineapple spears and peaches (grilling peaches is optional depending on how busy you are...nice touch if you have time). Butter pound cake slices and grill. After removing grilled pound cake, drizzle a tablespoon of rum over each slice.

Place grilled pineapple on a plate, lay a slice of pound cake on top of the pineapple. Drizzle **Caramel Rum Sauce** over grilled pound cake and garnish with a sliced and fanned strawberry. Serve with a dollop of fresh whipped cream or dairy-fresh homemade vanilla ice cream.

## CARAMEL RUM SAUCE

2 cups dark brown sugar

5 Tbsp. butter

1 cup heavy cream

1/4 cup Captain Morgan's Spiced Rum

3/4 cup sour cream

1/2 tsp. vanilla extract

1/4 tsp. cinnamon

Over medium high heat, melt brown sugar in a large 3-quart pan. Whisk until all the sugar has melted. **Be careful:** melted sugar can cause severe burns!

Add the butter and whisk until melted. Remove pan from heat. Add heavy cream and rum... whisk. The mixture will foam up—but keep stirring until blended.

Immediately add the sour cream, vanilla extract, and cinnamon and whisk to blend.

Kathy and I feeling "irie" in Cabo San Lucus.

# FAMOUS DAVE'S

## *Legendary*

### PARTY DRINKS & MOONSHINE

**PARTY LIKE IT'S PROHIBITION!**

# TABLE OF CONTENTS

## Party-Drink-Notes:

These party drink recipes feature one of America's most notorious and celebrated home-grown beverages…MOONSHINE! Today, there are legal moonshine distilleries that are producing mighty-fine hand-crafted, single-batch shine that would make any backwoods moonshiner proud. Now that moonshine is legal, folks are discovering that it is an all-around great enhancement to any party drink. It can take the place of vodka, gin, tequila, rum, or any whiskey, allowing the drink to be more flavorful. For instance, the Margarita made with moonshine will be the best you've ever tasted! The moonshine used in these recipes is not the 150-proof atomic throat burners but sippin' smooth 80-proof.

Pretty much all alcohol party drinks in this section can be served alcohol-free.

Please be creative… a person's beverage of choice can get pretty personal… and we encourage you to be creative in discovering tasty combinations of all the incredible fruit juices, flavored lemonades and teas, herbs and flavored concentrates available today. People taste with their eyes and little touches like creative garnishes can add excitement to your party.

One thing you will notice is that several recipes call for Black Raspberry Preserves. Whoever thought of mixing jam into a cocktail? Here's the deal…many recipes call for simple syrup, which is nothing but water and sugar. Why just add sugar when you can add fruit sugars or jam? We have attempted to incorporate Fruit Juice Concentrates, clover honey, and light agave honey in the place of simple syrup wherever possible. Have fun and be creative. Let your taste buds go wild. The recipes here are only a starting point to jumpstart your imagination!

# Peachy Mango Madness

**Here's a light, refreshing fruity cocktail that will have you looking for your thong!** Mangos, pineapple, oranges, with a splash of peach nectar, and smoothed out with sippin' smooth moonshine makes the perfect summer refresher!

### Serves a beach party of 3

1/2 cup mango juice

2 oranges, squeezed

1/2 oz. lime juice

2 oz. moonshine

1-1/2 cups pineapple slices

1 cup Kern's peach nectar

2 oz. light agave honey

7UP

Combine mango juice, pineapple slices, orange juice, peach nectar, lime juice, agave honey, and moonshine in a blender. Blend until smooth. Pour over ice and splash with 7UP and garnish with a pineapple wedge.

# Once in a Blue Moon

You won't have to wait for a blue moon with this refreshing blueberry-spiked drink. Whether it's a sunny spring day or sittin' on the front porch on a hot summer's day with friends, you're gonna luv this fruity country-inspired drink.

---

### Delightfully serves a party of 2

1/2 fresh orange, squeezed

4 oz. apple juice concentrate

4 Tbsp. Dickenson's Black Raspberry preserves

1 cup ice per serving

splash of 7UP

4 oz. fresh pineapple juice

3 oz. moonshine

1/4 lemon wedge

fresh blueberries

Combine fresh orange juice, pineapple juice, apple juice concentrate, moonshine, black raspberry preserves, and ice in a shaker. Squeeze a 1/4 lemon wedge into shaker. Shake vigorously and pour over ice into a chilled mason jar. Mix in fresh blueberries and splash with 7UP. Garnish with blueberries, fresh mint leaves, and lemon wheel. Just one word of caution: unless you want to look like you just fell off a hay wagon, don't be tempted to crush the blueberries—you'll end up with teeth full of tiny blueberry seeds!

# Bodacious Strawberry Blaster

A summer party in a glass any time of the year! You're gonna luv it... something new, a perfect fruity fresh drink that will get the party started.

## Serves a party of 2 good friends

3 mint leaves, torn and rubbed

2 strawberries

1/2 oz. fresh lemon juice

1 sliced large strawberry

1-1/2 oz. strawberry daiquiri margarita mix

1/2 oz. moonshine

1/2 oz. peach schnapps

splash Sprite

Muddle mint, strawberries, and lemon juice in a shaker. Add strawberry daiquiri margarita mix, peach schnapps, and moonshine. Shake vigorously and pour into a chilled, ice-filled mason jar. Splash with Sprite. Garnish with strawberry slices and mint leaves.

# SWEET STINGER

**Here's one honey of a drink!** More commonly known as an Arnie Palmer or a summery combination of the best two summer drinks: 50% ice tea and 50% lemonade that's been fizzed up with ginger ale and stung with moonshine!

## Delightfully stings a party of 1

1/2 cup hot tea

clover honey to taste

splash of ginger ale

1 cup ice

1/2 cup fresh-squeezed lemonade

1.5 oz. moonshine

1/2 lemon

Make your fresh-brewed ice tea and, while hot, sweeten with clover honey. Make your tea sweet enough to sweeten your lemonade. Combine sweet tea, sweetened lemonade, and moonshine along with ice in a shaker. Shake vigorously and pour over ice into a chilled mason jar. Splash with ginger ale and float a squeeze of fresh lemon juice on top...garnish with a lemon wedge. *Note: the honey stick is for picture only. Don't try to add honey to a cold drink—it won't work! Your honey has to be completely mixed with the hot tea.*

# BLOODY MARY'S

## BBQ PARTY IN A GLASS

When I am out traveling around, I often get many people who come up to me and tell me how much they love our barbecue ribs, but then I have to admit my Bloody Mary mix is my second-most-requested recipe and it is amazingly delicious without the booze. However, if you want to kick up the party—add a shot or two of moonshine to your glass!

**Delightfully wakes up a party of 6**

4 cups V8 Vegetable Juice

6 oz. Contadina Tomato Paste

1/2 cup Famous Dave's Devil's Spit

1 Tbsp. fresh lemon juice

1 Tbsp. fresh lime juice

1 Tbsp. ground horseradish (not prepared sauce)

1 tablespoon Pickapeppa Sauce

1/2 teaspoon celery salt

Garnishes: go hog wild!

Mix all the ingredients together in a pitcher. Salt the rim of your glasses. Pour Bloody Mary mix over a glass of ice and go hog wild on garnishes!

**Garnish Ideas:** One skewer has a Smoked Brisket chunk, pepperoncini pepper, Slim Jim, and grilled shrimp. The other skewer has a pearl onion, cherry tomato, pimento-stuffed green olive, black olive and a carved cherry tomato stuffed with a pearl onion. This Bloody Mary is finished with a pickle spear and a celery heart spear.

**Salting the Rim of the Glass:** mix celery salt with an equal portion of your best rib rub. For parties, it's best to salt the rim ahead of time. I use a heavy simple syrup that I place in a plate and stick my glass into this first and then into the celery salt and rib rub mixture. I let the glass sit for a while until the simple syrup dries and then the salted rim won't flake off. The rib rub gives the rim of the glass an unexpected flavor surprise!

# MARGARITA'S SPICY KISS

**Ole! Ole! It's always a hot time South of the Border and this Jalapeño Margarita's sure to add the spice to your party!** The adventurous kick of heat and the moonshine will make this jalapeño Margarita your new all time favorite. It's a real Fiesta in a glass!

**Kisses a party of 1**

1-1/2 oz. moonshine

1/2 oz. triple sec

Jalapeño, sliced

3 oz. margarita mix

splash of fresh-squeezed orange juice

coarse sea salt, lime slices, jalapeño slices for garnish

Prepare your mason jar glass by running a slice of lime along the rim and dipping the glass in coarse sea salt. When ready to serve, combine ingredients in a shaker with ice. Shake vigorously, and pour into glass and splash with orange juice. Garnish with sliced limes and jalapeño slices, and a whole jalapeño!

## Famous Dave's Hot Tips!

Combine as much moonshine, triple sec, margarita mix, and jalapeño slices in a pitcher as you will need for the drinks you will be serving. Refrigerate for 24 hours to let the jalapeño slices kick up the spiciness in the margarita mix.

# Sweetie Pie Fruit Punch

**Real southern hospitality... front porch sippin' style.** This is a fun, fruit-filled sweet tea that's been spiked to put the glow in your cheeks!

## Serves a sippin' party of 6

4 cups sweet tea

1/4 cup pineapple juice concentrate

1/4 cup orange juice concentrate

1/4 cup lemonade juice concentrate

1/2 cup Kern's Peach Juice

1-1/2 cup club soda or lemon-lime soda

1/2 fresh pineapple, sliced and chunked

1/2 orange, sliced into wedges

1/2 lemon, sliced into wheels

1 peach, sliced into wedges

1 cup moonshine

In a large pitcher, combine sweet tea, pineapple juice, orange juice, and lemonade concentrates, Kern's Peach Juice, and moonshine; stir well. Refrigerate until needed. Add pineapple chunks, orange, lemon, and peach wedges, club soda, and ice just before serving.

# BLACKBERRY SHINE

Blackberries always grow best in the shade where it's cool, and this mellow blackberry moonshine cocktail is sure to refresh and cool your taste buds silly!

## Puts the shine in a party of 1

4 blackberries

10 mint leaves, torn and rubbed

2 oz. Tbsp. Dickenson's Blackberry Preserves

1 oz. apple juice concentrate

1 oz. fresh lemon juice

1-1/2 oz. moonshine

1-1/2 oz. Chambord

1 cup ice

splash club soda

Blackberries and mint for garnish

Muddle blackberries, mint, and apple juice concentrate in a shaker. Add remaining ingredients, except club soda, to shaker and shake vigorously. Pour over ice in a chilled mason jar, splash with club soda, and garnish with a blackberry and mint leaves.

# Sangsational Sangria Punch

**Sometimes you need a chilling refreshing blast to celebrate the fun times... and this Sangsational Sangria packs the perfect fruity punch.** You're going to love this Sangria recipe as it also makes a lively & colorful centerpiece for any party table!

### Delights a party of 4 friends

1 bottle of your favorite red or white wine

1 peach

1 nectarine

1 orange

1 cup raspberries (frozen or fresh)

4.5 oz. peach schnapps

1-1/2 cans Sprite

Slice peach, nectarine, orange and orange into wedges. In a large pitcher combine red wine, peach, nectarine, orange, raspberries, and peach schnapps. Refrigerate for 1 hour (or up to 1 day). Add Sprite just before serving. Serve chilled over ice.

# Bonus Recipes...

## The Dunwoody Old Fashioned

**Orphaned at age 12, William Dunwoody traveled from Belfast to American in the late 1800s where he started smoking meats for Swift and Company.** Also a whiskey lover, William's love for good food and a good old fashioned has been passed on for generations at the Dunwoody backyard barbecues.

### Serves a party of 1

2 oz. moonshine

4 dashes Angostura bitters

1 tsp. maraschino cherry juice

1 tsp. sugar

1 orange wedge

splash of water

1 Cherry Blaster

In a mason jar filled with ice, add moonshine, bitters, maraschino cherry juice, and sugar. Squeeze orange wedge into drink and add the wedge. Splash with water and garnish with a Cherry Blaster.

## Cherry Blasters

Take a jar of maraschino cherries, pour out the syrup and replace with moonshine. Let the cherries soak for at least 2 hours before serving. Store them in your refrigerator for whenever you need to blast a party drink!

## The Cherry Whiskito Mojito

**This cherry mojito has been hijacked by moonshine and blended up into a drink so delicious you'll slap a mosquito and exclaim "Whiskito! That's good!"**

### Serves a Party of 2

1 cup frozen cherries, slightly thawed

8 mint leaves

3 oz. moonshine

1/2 lime, squeezed

1-1/2 cups ice

splash ginger ale

2 Cherry Blasters

In a blender, add cherries, mint, moonshine, squeezed lime juice, and ice. Blend until smooth. Pour into a chilled mason jar and splash with ginger ale. Garnish with a Cherry Blaster and mint leaves.

237

# Sunshine Refresher

Here's proof that the sun loves a good party... sun-ripened grapefruit, citrusy lemon and a late-night kiss of moonshine!

**Refreshes a party of 2**

2 oz. simple syrup

1 oz. lemon juice

4 oz. moonshine

2 dashes Angostura bitters

1.5 oz. grapefruit juice

2 oz. club soda

lemon rind twists

grapefruit slices

In a large glass, combine simple syrup, bitters, moonshine, lemon juice, and grapefruit juice, and stir. Pour over ice into a chilled mason jar and add club soda. Garnish with fresh grapefruit slices and lemon rind twists.

# TROPICAL MOON

Celebrate the tropical breezes of the islands and imagine you're a thirsty castaway just found by a group of party-loving islanders… fire up the tiki torches!

**Makes an island party of 4 feel "irie"**

6 fresh pineapples, cored

12 oz. fresh-squeezed orange juice

1 can frozen lemonade

2 cups purified water

1 ltr. 7UP

6 cups fresh pineapple juice

12 oz. peach schnapps

1 can frozen cranberry juice concentrate

1 cup moonshine

**Cherry Blasters** (pg. 237)

Slice tops off pineapples and save pineapple leaves for garnishes. Using a pineapple corer, remove the inside of the pineapple and puree in a food processor. Strain puree for 6 cups of juice. Combine pineapple juice, orange juice, cranberry concentrate, lemonade concentrate, water, peach schnapps, and moonshine; chill. For each pineapple, crush two cups of ice and mound in pineapple shell. Right before serving, add 7UP to the moonshine mix and pour over crushed ice. The crazier your garnishes… the more fun your drink will be!

# DIXIE'S WATERMELON PUNCH!

**Here's a fun way to serve a festive party punch.** A carved watermelon punch bowl and carved smaller watermelons for individual drink holders add homespun fun that makes the punch all that more flavorful!!!

## Serves a thirsty party of 8

1 qt. watermelon puree

1 can frozen lemonade concentrate

2 cans pure water

1 pint of strawberries, sliced

1 pint of raspberries

6 or 8 personal-size watermelons

16 ounces peach juice

1 can frozen cranberry cocktail concentrate

1 liter Sprite or 7UP

1 pint of blueberries

1 large watermelon

1 gallon rainbow sorbet

Carve large watermelon and save pulp. Carve small watermelons for individual drinks. Slice a thin section off the bottom of the watermelons to steady them, but be careful you don't slice into the fruit so they don't leak. Add watermelon puree, peach juice, lemonade, cranberry cocktail juice, and water together and chill. Chill Sprite. When you're ready for your party, add enough punch to your carved watermelon, then add scoops of sorbet. Splash with Sprite and garnish with fresh fruit.

# Watermelon Crawling in the Moonlight

Old fashioned watermelon punch is perfect for celebrating summer block parties, fun backyard BBQ parties, and butt rockin' country jam fests. There's nothing more refreshing than watermelon punch served up with a kick of moonshine.

## Refreshes a party of 1

1/2 cup watermelon, blended

1/2 oz. light agave honey

1/2 cup ice

Cherry Blasters (pg. 237)

1/2 cup lemonade

2 oz. moonshine

**7UP**

Place blended watermelon, lemonade, agave honey, moonshine, and ice in a shaker. Shake vigorously and pour over ice into a chilled mason jar. Splash with 7UP. Garnish with watermelon cubes and a watermelon slice on the rim. Don't forget a few **Cherry Blasters**. Cherry Blasters are maraschino cherries marinated in moonshine!

*Please enjoy your sippin' responsibly... or you'll end up doing the Watermelon Crawl back home!*

# FAMOUS DAVE'S

*Legendary*

## RESOURCES

### THE PASSION IS IN THE DETAILS

EAT ★ LAUGH ★ PARTY

# TABLE OF CONTENTS

# How To Barbecue & Grill

There are countless websites where you can learn all you want about barbecue. These are a few that I like to frequent for barbecue and party ideas.

Amazing Ribs – www.amazingribs.com
The Science of BBQ & Grilling

Barbecue'n On The Internet – www.barbecuen.com
The leading edge in outdoor cooking

BBQ Backyard – www.bbqbackyard.com
BBQ Pitmaster Social Network

BBQ Junkie – www.bbqjunkie.com
BBQ Recipes, Competitions, Joints, and Reviews

BBQ Pit Boys – www.bbqpitboys.com
Old-Time Barbecue & Grilling

BBQ Super Stars – www.bbqsuperstars.com
Where Barbeque Lovers Strut Their Stuff

Kingsford – www.grilling.com
Grilling Recipes & Menu Ideas

Celebrations – www.celebrations.com
Barbeque Recipes, Tips, Grilling, & Party Ideas

Grilling with Rich – www.grillingwithrich.com
The Latest BBQ & Grilling News

How To BBQ Right – www.howtobbqright.com
Recipes, videos, and methods from Competition BBQ

The BBQ Brethren – www.bbq-brethren.com
From The Backyard to the American Royal

The Smoke Ring – www.thesmokering.com
Everything BBQ

The Firepit and Grilling Guru – www.firepit-and-grilling-guru.com Firepits, Grills, Barbeques, and Fireplaces

---

## Creating the WOW Factor

There are great websites out there to find fun party lighting and decorations without busting the party budget. These are a few of my go-to sites for decorations and my "Famous" party touches.

americansale.com
bronners.com
target.com
snedcowholesale.com
wholesaleforeveryone.com

## Smokers For Home, Catering, & Competitions

When I first started my quest to make the World's Best Ribs… my smoker was nothing more than a galvanized garbage can. Today, there are many fine companies that make pretty good grills and smokers. Below are a few I have personally used at one time or another and recommend. I never recommend anything I haven't used.

BBQ Pits by Klose – www.bbqpits.com
Big Green Egg – www.biggreenegg.com
Cookshack – www.cookshack.com
Jack's Old South Cookers – www.jacksoldsouthsmokers.com
Jambopits – www.jambopits.com
Meadow Creek Smokers – www.meadowcreekbarbecue.com
Southern Pride – www.southernpride.com
Weber & Weber Smokey Mountain Cooker – www.weber.com

## Barbecue Organizations

There are numerous organizations dedicated to promoting the world of barbecue. My recommendation is to go to The BBQ Brethren website, find an organization close to your home, and get involved. Anyone interested in barbecue competitions should attend the annual conferences for the national organizations below.

The National Barbecue Association – www.nbbqa.com

Kansas City Barbeque Society – www.kcbs.com

## Publications Devoted To The World Of Barbecue

National Barbecue News
www.barbecuenews.com

Kansas City Bullsheet
www.kcbs.com

The BBQ Times
www.bqtimes.com

Fiery Food & BBQ
www.fiery-foods.com

The recommendations provided are my personal recommendations. These are not paid endorsements. My whole purpose is to help you create the Best Backyard Barbecue Party Ever!

~ "Famous Dave"

# A Pitmaster's Pantry of Secret Ingredients... REVEALED!

**NOTICE:** Most folks glancing at this list of ingredients will think… "Oh this is just a list of things I already have in my seasoning cabinet." NO, there is a very specific reason why I detailed out these ingredients… these ingredients all have their own flavor nuances or "tricks" that make a huge difference in how your final recipe turns out. For instance, if a recipe calls for pepper… I may use two types of grinds of pepper…fine grind will flavor all of the food and a coarse grind will be more pronounced initally with the chewing of the food. Similarly, canning salt is a very fine salt that flavors all of the food and a coarse grind salt will have a tendency to sit on top and will give you that salty first bite.

The following matrix of ingredients provides insight into the major flavor categories necessary to understand all the intricate flavor nuances used in the making of flavorful and great-tasting recipes. Primarily, these ingredients are the foundation for barbeque rubs, marinades, and sauces. The tricky part is understanding how much of each ingredient to add so that the flavor either commands instant taste bud recognition or is used subtly to enhance the flavor of another ingredient. This blending of ingredients almost takes on mystical potion-blending magic where you have to experiment to create your own signature flavor profile.

Just adding a seasoning to a recipe is basic, but when you start understanding all of the nuances, grinds, and temperatures to make a spice release its flavors… then you will create amazing "tastes" that will rock your food world and delightly WOW your family and friends.

## All Seasonings Are Not Created Equal

Just as important as the amount of an ingredient used when creating a certain flavor profile is the size of the grind, and whether it is fresh or dry, cooked or not cooked. And even at what temperature to add a seasoning all needs to be considered in order to achieve the perfect "taste." Then there is country of origin…for instance, oregano from Mexico is totally different in taste than Greek oregano. And paprika grown in Hungry is very different from paprika that is grown in Spain. This knowledge is what it takes to master the art of flavoring food. It's all about the love of enjoying flavorful food.

Near the end, I have included a list of secret ingredients that may surprise you, but are very common knowledge to most old-time barbeque pitmasters. They are used in varying degrees to kick-up any barbeque recipe, but it takes years of mistakes and wasted ingredients to gain the knowledge on how to use these secret ingredients.

## BASES FOR BARBECUE TYPE RECIPES

**WATER**
Only purified, filtered water will do. Pure filtered water will allow the natural flavors of your ingredients to be fully utilized throughout your recipe. Tap water is often treated with a variety of chemicals like chlorine and fluorides, and soft water is treated with salt. In addition, many city or rural water sources are considered "hard water" heavy with many minerals and sediment. For best results, run your tap water through a filter. The cleaner your water, the more flavor you will get out of your ingredients and the better your food will taste!

**KETCHUP**
This is an old standby for making quick and easy BBQ sauces. You don't want to skimp on quality here as the cheap stuff tends to break down easily. I always buy Heinz.

**TOMATO SAUCE**
This is OK, but tomato sauces tend to have other ingredients and you need to taste test the right sauce for your recipe. Tomato sauces are also thin and watery, which may be good or bad depending on regional tastes. I would much rather start from tomato paste so I can control the outcome of the flavor.

**TOMATO PASTE**
This is my favorite base and I prefer a good, concentrated tomato paste—usually Contadina or Hunt's—because the tomato flavors are really intense.

| | |
|---|---|
| **MUSTARDS** | Mustards are a great barbeque flavor base, but generally this is a regional East Coast preference. I have found that mustards can be tricky and you need to really taste test the different varieties to find the right mustard for your recipe. Most old-fashioned barbeque recipes use simple yellow mustard. |
| **VINEGARS** | Vinegars are usually an East Coast flavor base for BBQ sauces and they come in two major types: white vinegar and apple cider vinegar. I like getting creative and often will try a Rice Wine Vinegar or the fuller-flavored Balsamic Vinegar. |

## SWEETENERS

| | |
|---|---|
| **WHITE SUGAR** | A good sweetener where you don't want the sweetener interfering with the other ingredients. |
| **BROWN SUGAR** | Probably the most widely used sweetener in pitmaster-type barbeque sauces. Brown sugar has a rich carmelizing-type undertone. |
| **TURBINADO SUGAR** | I like this sugar as in its raw form. It is a much larger crystal than table sugar or brown sugars. Table sugar and brown sugar will melt more quickly during cooking, while Turbinado Sugar or Raw Sugar (same thing) should still have substance—giving your recipe a nice sugary crunch. I use this a lot on my smoked meats as this sugar helps create nice flavorful "bark." |
| **HONEY** | Many people like honey in their barbeque recipes and sauces but really don't know why. In addition to having a really smooth tasty natural flavor, honey has a magnifying quality that enriches the flavors of other ingredients, especially spices. Not all honey is the same… I have found that the best honey to use is a clover honey. Make sure you get real 100% honey… some honey is mixed with high fructose corn syrup—which you absolutely don't want. |
| **LIGHT AGAVE HONEY** | Sometimes clover honey can be too overwhelming and you need a subtle flavor boost that sugar can't achieve and this is where I have found that Light Agave Honey is just perfect! |
| **MOLASSES** | I prefer molasses as the heart and soul of a really great barbeque sauce. Molasses imparts a hearty carmelized flavor that mixes well with tomato-based sauces and blends well with smoke. There are a few varieties of molasses available: Blackstrap (which I find is sometimes a little bit too sharp like licorice), Light molasses (which is too light), and Full-Flavored, (which for me is the best choice). Additionally, I have found the most pleasant-tasting molasses is Grandma's unsulfured brand molasses. |
| **CORN SYRUP** | Corn Syrup is a common sweetener, but I have found that most corn syrups are blended with vanilla and you want to make sure the corn syrup you use is best for your palate. Karo is the best brand corn syrup sweetener for sweetening my barbeque sauces. Additionally, Karo makes a Dark Corn Syrup, which I prefer to use in my sauces because of the rich flavor. |
| **OTHER SWEETENERS** | Maple Syrup, Dr. Pepper, Coca Cola, Turbinado or raw sugar, and natural fruit juices. |

## WORCESTERSHIRE SAUCE

There is only one brand of Worcestershire sauce and that is LEA & PERRINS. There are other brands, but none has the intensity of flavor like Lea & Perrins. However, when I need a more subtle flavor, I use French's Worcestershire Sauce.

# FRUITS or FRUIT JUICES

**PINEAPPLE**       I love fresh pineapple juice for barbeque sauces. It has a nice fresh sweetening ability that doesn't take away from the other ingredients. Pureed pineapple will give some body to salsa-like barbeque sauces. I like grilling pineapple for plate garnishes.

**LEMONS**          Great citrus fruit juice with a freshness that gives any sauce some zip!

**LIMES**           Same pucker-up type power like lemon juice but its tartness adds an interesting flavor nuance to the sauce.

**ORANGES**         This is a nice mild citrus juice and is more likely to be used in milder sauces or glazes.

**APPLE JUICE**     Nice natural flavor but sometimes too mild. Although, it is good for spritzing on your barbeque while your meats are smoking. When I need a fuller robust apple flavor, I will use straight apple juice concentrate.

**OTHER FRUITS**    Tangerines, raisins, blueberries, raspberries, blackberries, grapes

# VINEGARS AS A FLAVOR BOOST FOR ALL RECIPES (most common forms)

**WHITE VINEGAR**   Creates tartness, which helps to wake up flavors.

**APPLE CIDER VINEGAR**   Doesn't quite give a sharp tartness to the taste buds like white vinegar and tastes more "earthy."

**BALSAMIC VINEGAR**   A very tasty aged wine vinegar that is a little sweet, with great body and carmelized fruity flavor nuances. The product I like the most and is most affordable for making a batch of sauce is Alessi Balsamic Vinegar Di Modena. Balsamic Vinegar is a great compliment to a molasses-flavored barbeque sauce.

**RICE WINE VINEGAR**   Nice and mild, with a little sweetness. Use rice wine vinegar for milder sauces.

**MALT VINEGAR**    Made from barley, malt vinegar has almost a caramel flavor and can provide a nice rich flavor.

# SALTS

**IODIZED TABLE SALT**   An OK salt but has chemical sharpness to it… however, it does its job.

**KOSHER SALT**     Preferred by most chefs. It is a coarse salt that has a subtle earthiness to it.

**SEA SALT**        I personally prefer sea salt. It has more natural saltiness to it without being overly sharp to the taste buds.

**OTHER SALTS**     There are other salts combined with seasonings like Onion Salt, Garlic Salt, and Celery Salt. While I prefer to use the pure spice and add salt, there are times like in a RIB RUB where one of these other salts actually works better to carry the flavor intensity.

# PEPPERS

**BLACK, FINE GRIND**   Black pepper (usually defined under "Spices" in the ingredient listing on a bottled sauce) is one of the best ingredients to give a Sauce its natural spiciness. I have also listed several other types of grinds available because the larger the grind the more peppery flavor they will provide to a sauce. I like using a finer grind black pepper because it infuses itself right into the sauce, compared to a cracked black pepper, which still retains its peppery flavor.

| **BLACK, COARSE GRIND** | A larger grain than fine grind but it pretty much is used for providing a burst of flavor when bitten into in a recipe. |
|---|---|
| **CRACKED BLACK** | Cracked black pepper actually will give a taste bud awakening when bitten into and I like using this larger grain for my bolder sauces. Cracked pepper gives a huge "up front in the mouth" pepper taste. |

**NOTE ABOUT BLACK PEPPER:** *Sometimes I will use all three grinds in a sauce to give a variety of pepper flavor nuances. The fine grind will bathe the entire mouth while the larger grinds, including cracked, will have intense pepper bursts only when bitten into.*

| **CAYENNE** | Has a cleaner hot spiciness that does not associate itself with the flavor of black pepper. I usually like to use this in combination with red pepper flakes. |
|---|---|
| **RED PEPPER FLAKES** | I like using red pepper flakes for the same reason I use cracked black pepper, they give an immediate flavor burst when bitten into. However, Red Pepper Flakes are more than just one kind of pepper; they are a combination of different peppers like cayennes, ancho chilis, and bell peppers. |
| **ALEPPO PEPPER** | This is a very interesting pepper that I like using in my more adventuresome recipes. It has ancho-like pepper undertones, but it also has mild citrusy nuances. It gives smoky barbeque really nice pepper sensations to the whole mouth, while not being too over powerful where the spice is uncomfortable. |
| **CHIPTOLE** | Sometimes I like using Chipotle peppers because of their subtle smokiness—as they are smoked jalapeños. These peppers are on the more spicy side. Comes either as a powder form or packed in adobo sauce. I prefer to buy the canned Chipotle in adobo sauce which I puree and keep in the refrigerator. |
| **FRESH JALAPEÑOS** | I like using fresh jalapeños because they have fresh veggie flavorings like their cousin the bell pepper. I tend to leave the seeds in because the seeds add a little bit more intensity to the hotness of the pepper. |
| **OTHER PEPPERS** | If you like a really hot sauce, there are many really hot peppers that will give your barbeque sauce a degree of hotness that would please even the devil himself! Some of these peppers include: Serranos, Scotch Bonnet, Habaneros, etc. |

**NOTE REGARDING HOT HOT PEPPERS:** *The only way that you can ever figure out how to make great-tasting barbeque recipes is that you have to learn the different flavor nuances of peppers. And there is only one way to get this understanding! You have to eat the peppers… don't worry—your tongue won't fall off or explode. Never use water to quench the heat of a fiery pepper that you just ate… use bread and milk. Water actually acts as a carrier and will spread the heat all over your mouth. Good Luck!*

## HOT PEPPER SAUCES

In the beginning of my barbeque experimentations, I would try adding hot pepper sauces to my recipes for adding "heat." I have since found that I could achieve better taste profiles by using the raw peppers without the vinegar masking the true flavor nuances of the pepper mash. However, these hot sauces do add their own personality to a BBQ recipe… so here are my thoughts on the most common hot sauces.

| **TABASCO** | Tabasco is probably the most commonly recognized name, but I am not a real big fan of this hot sauce only because it is very vinegary. If you compare this bottle of hot sauce to others on the market… it will appear very diluted. Its first taste is that of vinegar. For a big bold pepper taste, I would recommend one of the other sauces. |
|---|---|
| **LOUISIANA HOT SAUCE** | I like this sauce the best. It has a full spicy pepper taste and the vinegar is in perfect balance. I have found that this is a great sauce for splashing on your 'Que! |
| **FRANK'S RED HOT** | This is another common hot sauce, but its pepper profile doesn't seem as full-flavored as the Louisiana Hot Sauce. I still would choose this over Tabasco. |

| | |
|---|---|
| **CHOLULA HOT SAUCE** | If you are making a southwest barbeque sauce, I would definitely recommend using this sauce. Instead of the red pepper mash used in the above sauces, this Mexican sauce uses Arbol and Piquin peppers and you can definitely tell this sauce came from Mexico. |

## HERBS AND VEGETABLES

| | |
|---|---|
| **ONION, FRESH** | Depending on the intended flavor profile of the sauce, different onions can give sharp onion flavor or sweet onion flavor. |
| **ONION, POWDER** | I do not recommend you use this, because it is too fine and too much will turn your recipe mushy. |
| **ONION, GRANULATED** | I prefer to recommend this over onion powder. |
| **ONION, MINCED** | Minced Onions are dried flakes of onions. I don't like the size of flakes, but I like the retention of flavor found in the bigger pieces of onion. So I take the minced onion and grind it up in my coffee grinder. The resulting ground-up onion granules seems to work better in sauces and rib rubs. This extra step is well worth the effort for great onion flavor. |
| **GARLIC, FRESH CLOVES** | I love the use of fresh garlic, but this one flavor can get you in trouble because fresh garlic can really change the flavor of a sauce. Garlic in any form should be used as a subtle support flavor. Your barbecue recipes should never start tasting like Italian spaghetti sauce! When you do add fresh garlic, I recommend using a garlic press to get the best flavor possible. |
| **GARLIC, POWDER or GRANULATED** | The same holds true for garlic powder as onion powder. If I have to use garlic powder, I like the granulated stuff better. |
| **GARLIC, MINCED** | Other than fresh garlic cloves, I like Minced Garlic—I grind up the minced garlic in a coffee grinder and the resulting granules have a great taste that is full of flavor. |
| **HERBS** | Depending on the style of sauce needed for a particular cut of meat… sometimes I will use fresh herbs. If I can't find fresh then I will use new bottled herbs. I never keep bottled herbs longer than six months. These herbs include: Sweet Basil, Oregano, Rosemary, Thyme, etc. A sauce that uses these particular herbs also generally uses aromatic spices like nutmeg and cloves. Combinations of these seasonings for barbeque sauces require experimentation to get the flavors just right. However, these types of seasonings can give a sauce "depth" and interesting flavor profiles. Usually, I have found these flavorings used in sauces made in out-of-the-way, side street, storefront black-owned rib joints in Chicago, Memphis, or Kansas City. I am sure that these rich exotic flavor combinations date back to original African influences. |

## SPICES

| | |
|---|---|
| **CHILI POWDER** | Chili powder is a common spice used in many barbeque sauces. There are many varieties of chili powders. I have found it is important to buy a good chili powder because the taste will be richer and more full-bodied. Cheaper chili powders have a tendency to be "dusty." I also prefer to use a light chili powder compared to a dark chili powder, which can be too over-powering for the sauce… you don't want your barbeque sauce tasting like Chili! Chili powders also vary according to the amount of cumin and other blends of peppers that are used to make the chili powder. So, like any other seasoning, you have to make sure you know which brand best suits the flavor profile that you are trying to achieve in your sauce. |

| | |
|---|---|
| **ANCHO CHILE PEPPER** | Ancho chile pepper is a very mild chile that has a rich dark flavor and is used in Chili powders. This is also the base of Mexican dishes. It has a pure taste that does not confuse the palate with cumin like a chili powder. This is actually a great seasoning to use in all barbeque recipes. |
| **PAPRIKA** | Paprika is made from sweet red bell peppers. The best paprika I have found is Smoked Hungarian Paprika from Budapest. This is a very mild flavoring ingredient that is great for all barbeque recipes. |
| **DRY MUSTARD** | Dry mustard is made from grinding up yellow mustard seeds into a powder. It is the base for yellow prepared mustard that is commonly used on hot dogs. I have found that Colman's English Mustard is a good full-flavored dry mustard, but I do not use dry mustard if I am already using a prepared mustard in my sauce. Dry mustard has some heat qualities that are different than prepared yellow mustards and lends itself well for spicy sauces. |
| **CUMIN** | I like cumin in little amounts for barbeque sauces but it needs to be used sparingly—I find this is one of the spices that is best freshly ground in a coffee grinder. Cumin is an ingredient that gives chili powders and Mexican dishes their distinct southwest flavor. |
| **CELERY SEED** | This is a great addition to any barbeque sauce, as it has a nice wood-type flavoring. Over a smoky grill it picks up great barbeque flavoring, but use it sparingly. |
| **NUTMEG** | Grated nutmeg has a very unique flavor profile that gives an almost exotic taste to BBQ sauces. Use sparingly, you will not need much to change the entire flavor profile of a sauce. Sometimes this spice is more of a regional "acquired taste." Nutmeg—along with cloves—gives a good spicy depth to a sauce and makes the sauce more interesting. |
| **CLOVES** | Cloves are the aromatic flower buds of a certain type of tree. Like nutmeg, they have a very exotic flavor profile and should be used sparingly. I find the flavor is best if I grind up the cloves myself in my coffee grinder. |
| **JAMS AND PRESERVES** | Fruit jams and preserves make a great addition as an added surprise to any barbeque sauce. The natural fruit flavors sometimes will add just the right sweetness, pulpiness, and fruit tartness to a barbeque sauce. |
| **APRICOT PRESERVES** | I love to use apricot preserves in my sauces. The best apricot preserves will have a very noticeable tart bite, which lends itself well to any sauce. In addition, it combines very nicely with smoke! |
| **ORANGE MARMALADE** | This is a great addition to barbeque sauces, best used on smoky rotisserie chicken or turkey. |
| **CONCORD GRAPE JAM** | I love Concord grape jam as a last-minute addition to a freshly made batch of sauce. However, this jam works best in sauces that do not use molasses. |

## THICKENERS FOR BARBECUE SAUCES AND OTHER RECIPES

| | |
|---|---|
| **CORNSTARCH** | This works great, but you must bring your sauce up to boiling to get the starch to set. You also need to constantly stir your sauce or the cornstarch will make clear solid forms of set starch that do not incorporate into the sauce. You will need to experiment with how much cornstarch you will need to achieve the right thickness for your recipe. |
| **NATURAL THICKENERS** | For some barbeque sauces or recipes, I do not want a starchy feel, so I will often use pureed natural fruits as thickeners such as: pineapple pulp, apple pulp, raisin pulp, lemon pulp, lime pulp, and orange pulp. If you are making a BBQ sauce and you don't want a fruity-tasting sauce… just adding more tomato paste will also thicken up a sauce. |
| **REDUCTIONS** | I like reductions because you can really achieve a more intense flavor. Also, reductions are another way to thicken a recipe by reducing the watering in the recipe through low heat. This is sometimes preferred, as it also intensifies the flavors. |

| **XANTHUM GUM** | This is an interesting sauce thickener and sometimes it is hard to find in grocery stores, although you can find it online. Once you learn how to use this unique bi-product from corn syrup… you'll use it in your other recipes! |

## BOOZE

Although I personally quit drinking many long years ago, I still love cooking with booze. Full-flavored boozes or liqueurs lend themselves nicely to the addition of a sauce. There isn't anything better to add to a great barbeque sauce, than a little "nectar of the gods!"

Don't worry about the booze in the sauce; it will burn off as you cook your sauce leaving only the unique tasty nuances. The following is my choice of boozes for great-tasting barbeque sauces:

| **JACK DANIELS** | A good full-flavored Tennessee Whiskey. |
| **SOUTHERN COMFORT** | Fruity, spicy whiskey-type liqueur. |
| **PEACH SCHNAPPS** | The peach flavor works wonders with most barbeque sauces! |
| **APRICOT SCHNAPPS** | This is another good addition to any barbeque sauce. |
| **KAHLUA** | I like adding Kahlua to sauces because of its rich coffee and chocolate-like flavors. Kahlua and Apricot Preserves work well together and are terrific additions to any barbeque sauces. |
| **WINE REDUCTIONS** | Best used in simple barbeque recipes—especially on meats like smoked pork tenderloins. |
| **BEER** | Although some barbeque cooks swear by the addition of beer, I think it is better as a marinade for brats when grilling. I have a hard time using it for traditional barbequing with the one exception of chicken. For some reason, beer adds a nice flavor to smoky chicken. |

## OTHER PITMASTER SECRET FLAVOR INGREDIENTS

The following ingredients are a few BBQ Secrets that take experimentation to figure out, but in limited quantities, can sometimes add that little Zip, Zest, or Burst that makes a sauce or any other barbecue recipe unique in taste.

Semi-sweet Chocolate, Horseradish, Citric Acid, Teriyaki Sauce, Soy Sauce, Sweet Chili Sauce, Maggi Gravy Seasoning, Accent, Beef Base, Chicken Base, Liquid Smoke: Hickory or Apple Flavors, Lemon Peel, Sesame Seed Oil, Pan Drippings: Hickory-Smoked Bacon, Watermelon Juice Reductions, Raisin Juice Reductions, and Tamarind.

## BUYING YOUR SEASONINGS AT THE RIGHT PRICE

If you are going to be having an old fashioned Bar-B-Que and you will be doing up a whole bunch of ribs, buy your seasonings in bulk. Buying little bottles of herbs and spices in a grocery store can quickly become expensive. Buying your seasoning in bulk at Sam's Club or Wal-Mart can save you a bundle! For example: a little 2 oz. bottle of Black Pepper in a Grocery store was recently $2.54 and then I went to Sam's Club where I bought a 20oz. Restaurant-Size Container for $4.82. That means the grocery store pepper is $1.27 per ounce and the restaurant pepper is $0.24 per ounce… this is a huge savings!

# This Book is Dedicated to My Mom & Dad

This cookbook is dedicated to my Mom and Dad, both Native Americans, who gave me the passion for cooking great Southern food and the love for barbeque! My dad is from the Choctaw Nation, Idabel, Oklahoma, and my mom is from the Lac Courte Oreilles Lake Superior Band of Ojibway, Hayward, Wisconsin.

I can really say that I started out from humble beginnings. I learned how to cook for large groups of people from my mom's Indian Fry Bread Stand, a tarp-covered lean-to at American Indian Pow-Wows. It is from this tarp-covered stand that I would help my mom sell Indian Fry Bread, Wild Rice Soup and Venison Fry Bread Sandwiches to the Indian dancers and the tourists who came to watch these magnificent, historical, and colorful Indian Pow-Wows.

**"Jimmie" and Iris Anderson**

**Mom's Indian Fry Bread Stand at the Honor The Earth Pow-Wow on the Lac Courte Oreilles Indian Reservation, Hayward, Wisconsin. Circa the late 70s.**

Today, I affectionately say that my Mom's Indian Fry Bread Stand was really my first restaurant! It was from my Mom that I learned how to cook for large groups of people. My dad was born right smack in the middle the "Bible Belt" in Oklahoma and it was from my Dad where I learned how important the right ingredients were to creating robust, flavorful, tasty barbecue.

# This Book is Also Dedicated to all Raving Fans of Barbecue

This cookbook is also dedicated to all the folks who passionately love barbecues, parties, tailgating, or just plain having fun while cooking up some great-tasting barbecue. I also want to dedicate this book to all the folks who blog about barbecue, the folks who volunteer to organize BBQ competitions, the Kansas City Barbecue Society, the National Barbecue Association, all the vendors who make barbecuing possible, and most importantly all the raving loyal fans who love eating barbecue! I also want to dedicate this cookbook to my family... James & Colleen, and their two sons Miles & Cooper; and my other son, Timothy, who all helped taste test my recipes over the years. Finally, I want to dedicate this cookbook to all the folks at Famous Dave's who live for barbecue and passionately live the Famous Dave's brand every day. At Famous Dave's, we just don't make great-tasting barbecue, we live the brand. To us, barbecue is not just a food, but a culture—it is our way of life!

# Acknowledgments

Making a cookbook like this takes an incredible amount of work, planning, organizing, AND CLEANUP! I could not have even considered doing this cookbook without all the tireless help of my wife Kathy. Then there are the people who stood side by side with me through the tough times and the good times: Mark Lundeen, my helper and photographer. Lance Como & Cory Johnson who did the graphic and design work. Claire Terrones, who edited and helped keep me organized, which is no small task. And Cathy Bowlby, Jacie Poitra, and Scott Barber, who helped cook, clean, and organize all the stuff that it takes to create a food photo. Paul Fricke and Blue Moon Studios for my little Famous Dave caricatures. Doug Anderson and Deb Hatampa at Driven Revenue Marketing Group for a few key graphics. I also want to acknowledge Christopher O'Donnell, President of Famous Dave's, without Christopher's support this cookbook would not have been possible. Then there are Charlie Torgerson and Dan Conroy who work in the Food & Beverage department at Famous Dave's. I can't forget Ben & Barb Welshons, and Victor Salmone... from time to time, they all came over and helped chop & clean, but I suspect they were really anxious to taste-test my new recipes!

*Making a cookbook almost requires complete destruction of a kitchen and I am so blessed my wife keeps her cool and is understanding!!!*

*Claire Terrones, this remarkable woman keeps my world focused and organized!*

*Lance Como, graphic logistics
Cory Johnson, main graphic designer
www.comoltd.com*

*Karen D'Ascenzo,
in control of the grocery money!*

*One photograph can trash a whole kitchen and it may take making the same dish 10Xs until the food looks tasty enough you want to lick the page!*

*Cathie Bowlby made sure I had everything I was looking for!*

# Photo Credits

Mark Lundeen was the main photographer for all the food shots— including his invaluable help in keeping the BBQ pits stoked while I prepped food with my crew. Tim Steinberg, food shots and background pictures: www.timsteinberg.com; Gary Eckhart, bluesfest pictures, bluesmangary@gmail.com; Chuck Ryan bluesfest pictures: www.chuckryanphotography.com; Craig Bares, home party pictures: www.craigbares.com; and Scott Shulter from National Camera for helping me understand my camera. And Famous Dave for many of the "fill in" pictures!!!

# It takes a village to make a cookbook…
## I am so grateful for all our family & friend's help and passion!

**Cooper & Miles**
*World's Best Taste Testers!*

**Paul Rynning, Farm Fresh Veggies**
*"Making things grow is spiritual"*

**Colleen & Claire**
*My drink taste testers, "We love this job!"*

**Charlie Torgerson**
*Great Chef and Friend*

**Barb Welshons**
*"Hmm…I think you should add this!"*

**Jacie Poitra**
*"I can do anything!"*

**Dan Conroy**
*Great Chef and Friend*

**Scott Barber**
*"Let me help you… DONE!"*

**Cathie & Kathy**
*"Works done…Time To Party!"*

**Randy Ehlers**
*"Whatever you need, I'll get it… don't worry!"*

**Colleen, Nita, Tim**
*"You've got to be kidding…one more recipe?"*

**James**
*"Dad this is how its done!"*

254

Famous Dave's traveling rib team… "You've got to compete against the best to be the best!"

# INDEX

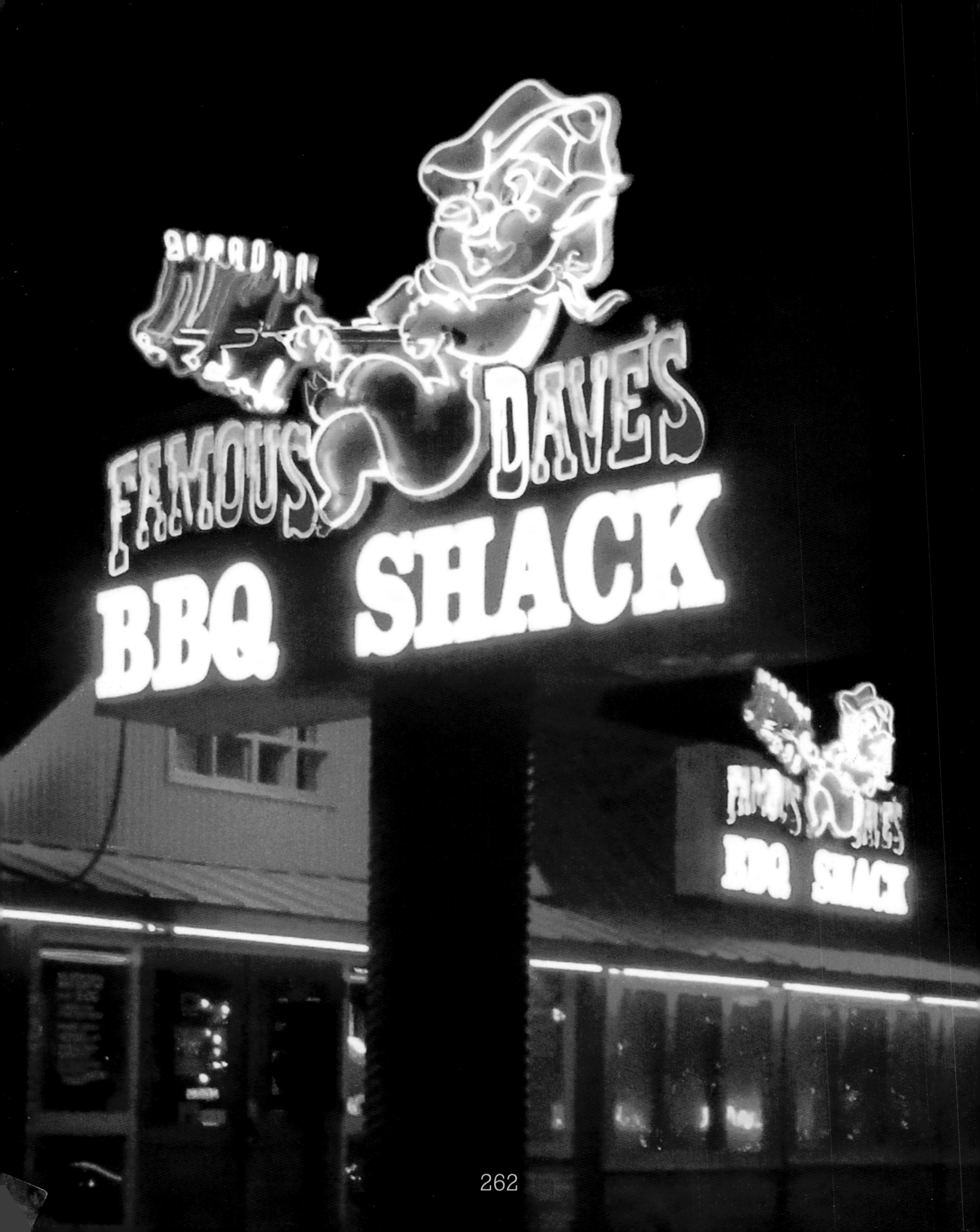
FAMOUS DAVE'S
BBQ SHACK
FAMOUS DAVE'S
BBQ SHACK

Thankyou Come Again HAVE A BLESSED DAY

Sign on a Nashville BBQ joint.

In Memory of a true Pitmaster, Butch Lupinetti, a BBQ Legend who won over 500 awards for his tasty barbecue. Butch traveled the U.S. and Canada serving his Smack Your Lips BBQ to thousands of BBQ loving fans. Butch never turned away a hungry mouth and was the most generous man I have known. I know today Butch is serving the Good Lord his tasty barbecue in Hog Heaven... Keep on Smokin'!